JORGE MARIO BERGOGLIO

POPE FRANCIS

IN HIM ALONE IS OUR HOPE

Spiritual Exercises
Given to His Brother Bishops
in the Manner of Saint Ignatius of Loyola

MAGNIFICAT

New York • Paris • Madrid • Oxford

Publisher: Pierre-Marie Dumont
Editor: Romain Lizé
Translation: Father Vincent Capuano, s.j., and Andrew Matt
Layout: Élise Borel and Georges Boudier
Copyediting: Andrew Matt
Proofreading: Janet Chevrier
Photo engraving: Aquatre
Production: Thierry Dubus and Gwendoline da Rocha

First edition: July 2013
ISBN : 978-1-936260-58-4

Photo Cover: © Reuters/Alessandro Bianchi

Printed in Canada by Marquis, July 2013
www.magnificat.com

TABLE OF CONTENTS

We are grateful to Pope Francis for having authorized us to publish this book. It is a document that offers great insight into the heart and concerns of the new Pope whom the Holy Spirit has just given to the Church and to the entire world. In particular, this text reveals how the Bishop of Rome, shepherd of the universal Church, understands the ecclesial mission of the shepherds of God's people.

✠ **Antonio María Rouco Varela**
Cardinal Archbishop of Madrid
President of the Spanish Episcopal Conference

Foreword

Seán Cardinal O'Malley, O.F.M. Cap.
Archbishop of Boston
May 29, 2013

Our Holy Father, Pope Francis, is a great blessing for all Catholics, especially Catholics from the Americas. He is the first pope from the American hemisphere and, being Hispanic, he is from a part of the world where almost half of all Catholics reside. Pope Francis is a man who has dedicated his ministry to the poor and to announcing the Gospel in difficult situations. In the first few months of his pontificate he has set a beautiful example, and he is urging us all to imitate him. During his first general audience he encouraged us to "move beyond a dull or mechanical way of living our faith, and instead open the doors of our hearts, our lives, our parishes, our movements or associations, going out in search of others so as to bring them the light and the joy of our faith in Christ."

It was a pleasure for me to visit him a few years ago. I had met him over the years on a number of different occasions, but had the joy of spending time with him in Buenos Aires, where he was serving as archbishop up until his election as pope in March of 2013. I had made a trip to South America for the United States Conference of Catholic Bishops to visit some projects that we were funding in Paraguay, and it was during this trip that I stopped in Argentina and was received as Cardinal Bergoglio's guest. It was a wonderful visit. I still cherish the beautiful recording of the *Missa Criolla*, the Argentine Mass, which he gave to me as a gift before I left. I did not encounter him again until we cardinals gathered in Rome to elect the new pope.

The conclave that elected Pope Francis was an experience of God's love for the Church and of the power of the Holy Spirit at work in the Church. It was a very emotional and moving moment when Cardinal Bergoglio accepted his election and announced that his name would be Francis in honor of saint Francis of Assisi. He said very explicitly that he was taking the name after saint Francis of Assisi. As a Jesuit, it would have been understandable if he had chosen the name in honor of saint Francis Xavier, who is one of the greatest missionaries in the history of the Church. But he chose to associate himself and his ministry with *Il Poverello*, the poor one.

Since his election as pope, Pope Francis has captured the spirit of saint Francis and has communicated some of the major themes from the life of the saint.

One of the themes of Francis' life is the call to rebuild the Church, which is a call to reform, and to deepen our conversion to the Lord. Another theme would be Francis' call to universal brotherhood; of making a world where we are brothers and sisters to each other. Saint Francis saw himself as a brother to everyone and even to all of creation. This is captured in the beautiful words of his canticle to *brother sun* and *sister moon*.

Saint Francis also had a special love for the poor, who are a sacrament of the crucified Christ. In his ministry as archbishop of Buenos Aires, Cardinal Bergoglio was dedicated to the poorest of the poor. I have every reason to believe that we will see a continuation of this in his pontificate.

After Pope Francis announced his name, we prayed the *Te Deum*, the traditional Catholic prayer of thanksgiving. The ballots were burnt, and the white smoke and bells announced to the city of Rome and to the entire world that the new pope had been elected. When we went out to the loggia overlooking the Square of saint Peter's Basilica, I was impressed by the sight of thousands of people cheering, waving flags, and taking pictures. The crowd erupted in applause when they saw the Holy Father for the first time.

His greeting to the people was warm and simple, and he asked us all to pray for him. He then bowed down as in complete silence we prayed for him and asked God to bless him. What happened next was most impressive: he led the people in praying the Our Father, the Hail Mary, and the Glory Be. This was a very moving moment for me because it occurred to me that these very simple prayers are the ones that every Catholic knows, regardless of education and training. People of all ages know these favorite prayers, which unite us as a Catholic people in our life of faith and worship of God.

We have been blessed in the last century and a half with so many exceptional and holy men who have led us in the Catholic Church, though each of them was so different from the one who came before. Someone once told me that the Italians have an expression — "After a fat pope, a thin pope" – which means that each one is different, each one has different gifts that they bring to their ministry in the Church.

Pope Francis continues the apostolic ministry of saint Peter, and he does so with a unique style and with gifts that will enable him to serve the people of God throughout the world. This book is a beautiful encounter with Pope Francis, in which we glimpse the gifts of his faith and his teaching. The lessons contained in these pages are an invitation for us to go ever deeper, to let our faith take firmer root, and to draw life from Christ, the wellspring of our salvation.

With gratitude to God for the election of Pope Francis, whose simplicity and joy are contagious, let us remember what he asked of all of us that night that he appeared on the loggia of saint Peter's when he asked us to pray for him. May God give him good health and fill him with joy as he continues the joyful witness of the successors of saint Peter and confirms us in our faith in Jesus Christ, who alone is our Hope. ■

SPIRITUAL EXERCISES
GIVEN TO HIS BROTHER BISHOPS
IN THE MANNER OF
SAINT IGNATIUS OF LOYOLA

My brothers, I would like to begin these Spiritual Exercises by citing a passage you yourselves penned at the close of this past century, a passage filled with profound consolation that echoes forth the *Magnificat*:

> What moves us most is the desire to thank God and to praise him, above all because *"his mercy is from age to age on those who fear him"* (Lk 1:50). We also feel called to conversion, impelled to ask for and receive pardon from God and joyful to renew our faith, our hope in his promises.[1]

As with Mary, our acts of thanksgiving, adoration, and praise found[2] our memory in the mercy of God that sustains us. With hope that is firmly rooted in him, we are thus prepared to fight the good fight of the faith and of love, on behalf of all those entrusted to our care.

---

1 *La fidelidad de Dios dura siempre. Mirada de fe al siglo XX* [God's faithfulness endures forever: A glance at the twentieth century through the eyes of faith]. Document approved by the 73rd Plenary Assembly of the Spanish Episcopal Conference, Madrid, November 26, 1999.

2 The verb "to found" *(fundar)*, which plays on the word "foundation," is one of the key terms Jorge Mario Bergoglio employs throughout this work. This term, which the author discusses at length in chapter 2 (The Lord Who Founds Us), refers specifically to the text from the beginning of the *Spiritual Exercises* of Saint Ignatius called the Principle and Foundation. (Editor's Note)

In order that we may readily receive the gift of hope as we begin these Spiritual Exercises, it is essential that we pray to the Holy Spirit. For he alone is the source of this gift, and only he can inscribe on our hearts all that is good.

This spiritual hope is much more than mere optimism. It is not full of fanfare, nor is it afraid of silence. Rather, it penetrates deep down within us, like sap in winter roots. Hope is certain, and it is the Father of Truth who gives it to us. Hope discerns between good and evil. It does not worship at the altar of success: falling into optimism; nor is it content with failure: wallowing in pessimism. Because hope discerns between good and evil, it is called to do combat. Yet it fights without anxiety or illusion, with the assurance of one who knows that he pursues a sure goal, as we read in the Bible: *"Let us lay aside every encumbrance of sin which clings to us and persevere in running the race which lies ahead"* (Heb 12:1). This is precisely how we wish to begin these Spiritual Exercises: asking for the grace of a combative hope.

The *Magnificat* versus institutional desperation

Since the combativeness of our hope is expressed above all in the work of discernment, we need to take an honest look at the attitudes of desperation that sometimes find a nest in the heart of institutions we belong to. These attitudes of desperation progress along the same steps as those that draw one under "the standard of the deadly enemy of our human nature" and his Anti-Kingdom:[3] they

---

3 In employing the term "Anti-Kingdom," the author alludes to the

begin with aversion to poverty, lead to vanity, and end in overweening pride (*Sp. Ex.*, 142).[4]

The Magnificat *is sung in poverty*

"The rich he has sent empty away" (Lk 1:53). Very often our lack of hope is a sign of hidden riches, the lack of evangelical poverty.

Thus, in confronting the scarcity of vocations, for example, we sometimes turn to the diagnostic techniques of the rich: rich in the knowledge of modern anthropological science. However, this wealth of scientific expertise, with its air of absolute self-sufficiency, often comes at the price of distancing us from the humble prayer of supplication and of dependence upon the Lord of the harvest.

Similarly, in the face of the magnitude and complexity of problems in the modern world, we often disguise the poverty of the solutions at our disposal as a kind of wealth, unaware that this supposed wealth consists solely in criticism and fault-finding. By trying to get rich with what is negative, we only succeed in acquiring rusty riches.

And we could continue enumerating similar examples.

Meditation on Two Standards proposed by Saint Ignatius in the second week of the *Spiritual Exercises*. The terms "Anti-Kingdom" and "Kingdom" do not appear in the Exercises, but rather two "standards" or banners: "the one of Christ, our supreme leader and Lord, and the other of Lucifer, the deadly enemy of our human nature" (no. 136). We cite here the words used by Saint Ignatius in the number of the Exercises to which Jorge Mario Bergoglio makes precise reference. —Ed.

4   All subsequent references to the *Spiritual Exercises* of Saint Ignatius will be indicated with the abbreviation *Sp. Ex.* —Ed.

It would be good during this retreat to bring our attachments to riches before the Lord in prayer, asking him to strip us of these attitudes toward wealth insofar as they are signs of desperation. Let us remember that the hope of the Kingdom comes with birth pangs.

The Magnificat *is sung in littleness and humiliation*

On soil that is not plowed by pain, the harvest is condemned in advance to insignificance (Lk 8:13). We are all beset by numerous vanities, but the most common kind, paradoxically, is defeatism. Defeatism is a form of vanity because one assumes the role of a general — but of a defeated army! — rather than accepting to be a simple soldier in a platoon, decimated though it may be, which continues to fight on.

How often do we bishops dream up our expansionist plans like defeated generals! In so doing, we deny the history of our Church that is a glorious history because it has been forged through sacrifices, hopes, and daily combat. The faith of our Fathers was passed on and blossomed in spite of precarious limitations and precious few human resources. Instead of becoming discouraged, however, our Forefathers pressed on with joy. Because their hope was stronger than every adversity.

The Magnificat *is sung in humility*

As we have just noted, pride leads us at times to denigrate the humble means of the Gospel. The following paragraph in the Constitutions of the Society of Jesus applies perfectly to today's Church. Saint Ignatius says:

The Society [or the Church] was not instituted by human means; and it is not through them that it can be preserved and increased, but through the grace of the omnipotent hand of Christ our God and Lord. Therefore in him alone must be placed the hope that he will preserve and carry forward what he designed to begin for his service and praise and for the aid of souls. (*Const.* 812)

If the Lord grants us the grace to live what Ignatius asks of us, then we will have attained the humility to consider ourselves faithful stewards, and not the Master of the house. We will be humble servants, like our Lady, and not princes. This humility is nourished through contempt and scorn, not flattery and self-satisfaction.

I would like to turn to the example of the wise virgins in the Gospel (Mt 25:1-13). This parable provides an essential lesson for the Church. You will recall that the wise virgins refused to share the oil for their lamps. A hasty and superficial reading would condemn them as stingy and selfish. A more profound reading reveals the grandeur of their attitude. These wise virgins do not share *what cannot be shared*.... They do not risk losing what should not be risked: the encounter with the Lord and what such an encounter is worth. It could happen, even in the Church, that we are treated with contempt and scorn for following the Lord, for refusing to "test the oxen," "buy the land," and "get married" (Lk 14:18-20).

In following in the footsteps of the Lord, our humility coincides with the practice of poverty, because poverty helps us draw close to what is essential. As a result, we discern what is fruitful and what isn't; we see through the lures of wealth. Because the life of God in us is not a luxury, but rather our daily bread, we must cultivate it with care through prayer and penance. This spirit of prayer and penance, even in the midst of great adversity, will guide us—alert and full of hope—along God's path.

II

THE LORD WHO FOUNDS US

At the beginning of his *Spiritual Exercises*, Saint Ignatius places us before Jesus Christ our Lord, our Creator and Savior:[5]

> Man is created to praise, reverence, and serve God our Lord, and by this means to save his soul. The other things on the face of the earth are created for man to help him in attaining the end for which he is created. Hence, man is to make use of them in as far as they help him in the attainment of his end, and he must rid himself of them in as far as they prove a hindrance to him. Therefore, we must make ourselves indifferent to all created things, as far as we are allowed free choice and are not under any prohibition. Consequently, as far as we are concerned, we should not prefer health to sickness, riches to poverty, honor to dishonor, a long life to a short life. The same holds for all other things. Our one desire and choice should be what is more conducive to the end for which we are created. (Principle and Foundation, *Sp. Ex.*, 23)

---

5   The following text, which is called the Principle and Foundation, is the first meditation proposed to those who make the *Spiritual Exercises* of Saint Ignatius Loyola. It lays out the fundamental attitudes that should guide a person who is seeking God's will: to recognize the end for which he or she has been created, namely, to praise, reverence, and serve God; to strive for "indifference" in relation to anything that does not lead to God; to know that this search will never end, that it will always involve seeking "more." Jorge Mario Bergoglio comments on the Principle and Foundation throughout this chapter, making frequent as well as creative use of this typically Ignatian vocabulary. —Ed.

Gazing upon the Lord

In this Principle and Foundation, when Saint Ignatius speaks to us about what our attitudes should be as saved creatures seeking their salvation, he presents us with the image of Christ, our creator and savior. And when he proposes a program of indifference and discreet generosity for choosing "what is more conducive" to this end, he presents us to "the ever greater God" *(Deus semper maior)*, to the One who is more intimate to me than I am to myself *(intimior intimo meo)*. This image of the *"Deus semper maior"* is distinctively Ignatian—it is what draws us out of ourselves and moves us to praise and reverence him; it fills us with the desire to follow him with greater love and to serve him better.[6] By this Lord and for him "man is created."

With Mary's gaze

The gaze of Mary in the *Magnificat* helps us to contemplate this ever greater Lord. The dynamic of this "more" *(magis)* inspires the rhythm of the *Magnificat*, which is the canticle of praise that humility sings to greatness.

This greatness of the Lord, contemplated with the pure eyes of Mary, purifies our gaze, purifies our memory in its two movements: that of "remembering" and that of "desiring."

The gaze of our Lady is combative when it comes to "remembering": nothing obscures or taints the past, the

---

6 "To choose what is more for the glory of his Divine Majesty" (*Sp. Ex.*, 152). It should be noted that the motto of the religious order founded by Saint Ignatius, the Society of Jesus, is: *Ad Majorem Dei Gloriam* (For the Greater Glory of God). —Ed.

great things that the Lord has done. He *has looked with favor on her lowliness*, and this first act of love is the foundation of her whole life. For this reason Mary's memory is a memory filled with gratitude.

With her, then, we gaze at our own beginnings or "principles,"[7] asking for the grace to discover in them how *the Lord loved us first* (for *love consists in this*, as Saint John says [cf. 1 Jn 4:10]).

In the light of Christ, *image of the invisible God, the first-born of all creation...[who] is before all things, and in him all things hold together* (Col 1:15, 17), we remember our first "principles" or beginnings:

- our beginning in God
- the beginning of our Christian life
- the beginning of our vocation
- the beginning of our priestly and episcopal life...

As we sing the canticle of the *Magnificat*, we feel the gaze of the Lord upon these beginnings in our life — a gaze that fortifies and founds us. And we pray that Mary's gaze may guide and strengthen our own, that with her we may keep our gaze fixed firmly upon the Lord.

The principle and foundation of our episcopal mission

From thanksgiving — the honor rendered to the Giver for the gifts he has bestowed — springs praise of the Lord.

---

7 Here the author plays on the double meaning of the word *principios* ("principles" or "beginnings"), while simultaneously alluding to the Principle and Foundation (*Sp. Ex.*, 23), cited above.

In this spirit of gratitude, let us pause now to consider the principle and foundation of our episcopal mission. We ask for the grace to identify ourselves ever more intimately with this mission. And we pray, in a very special way, that we may rediscover with the certitude of faith that we have been created and saved by the same Lord who now calls us to exercise "indifference" and to seek the discreet generosity of *greater service* in this specific mission.

The refusal of the mission

In this meditation you will feel the need to examine your own personal situation in relation to your episcopal mission:

- the hopes and the feelings of hopelessness
- the dreams and the disappointments
- the discouragements, prejudices...

I recommend that you review some of the typical phrases that form part of what we might call the "patois" of priests and bishops. It would be good to test their veracity before the Lord. I offer some examples, but each of you can add others as the Lord inspires you in prayer:

- What perhaps in the beginning was: "I'm not suited for that" may have changed into: "At this stage of the game I'm done with that."
- "This parish, this clergy, this diocese, makes me tired with all their complaints and demands."
- "Maybe I would work more effectively under different conditions."
- "If only my circumstances were better..."

In our humility we discover his greatness

For our consolation, Revelation has preserved the memory of the particular relationship between the Lord and the one whom he gives a mission: Moses, Isaiah, Jeremiah, John the Baptist, Joseph. Each one of them experiences profound inadequacy and unworthiness before the Lord's call:

> *"Who am I that I should go to Pharaoh and lead the Israelites out of Egypt?"* (Ex 3:11)
>
> *"Woe is me, I am doomed! For I am a man of unclean lips."* (Is 6:5)
>
> *"Ah, Lord God! I know not how to speak; I am too young."* (Jer 1:6)
>
> *"I need to be baptized by you, and yet you are coming to me?"* (Mt 3:14)
>
> *"Joseph decided to divorce her quietly. Such was his intention..."* (Mt 1:19-20).

This is the initial resistance, which may return from time to time — the fear of the mission, the inability of the one who is called to comprehend its magnitude. This is a sign of the good spirit, above all if one does not remain there but rather lets *the power of the Lord reveal itself in this weakness* and give him a foundation and consistency:

> *"I will be with you; and this shall be your proof that it is I who have sent you: when you bring my people out of Egypt, you will worship God on this very mountain."* (Ex 3:12)
>
> *"See, now that this has touched your lips, your wickedness is removed, your sin purged."* (Is 6:7)

"Say not, 'I am too young.' To whomever I send you, you shall go; whatever I command you, you shall speak. Have no fear before them, because I am with you to deliver you." (Jer 1:7-8)
"Allow it now, for thus it is fitting for us to fulfill all righteousness." (Mt 3:15)
"Joseph, son of David, have no fear about taking Mary as your wife. It is by the Holy Spirit that she has conceived this child." (Mt 1:20)

Founded in our belonging to the Church

When the Lord gives us our mission, he founds our being. He does not do so in a merely functional way, like one who gives someone a job or occupation. Rather he does it with the power of his Spirit, in such a way that we belong to the mission and our very identity is indelibly marked by it.

To identify with something means to belong to it. Thus, to belong means to participate in what Jesus founds; and Jesus founds us in his Church, in his holy and faithful people, for the glory of the Father. Our episcopal "patois" is perhaps born of the same sentiment that initially moved Moses, Isaiah, and John to recoil before their own missions. If this is the case, then let us allow the Lord to speak to us and gather up our fear, our pusillanimity, our egoism, into his greater plan.

Becoming formed and rooted in the Church

In a discussion about the so-called "base communities," Pope Paul VI offers us the foundational criteria that Jesus wanted for his Church. These criteria can shed light on our contemporary situation and our examination of conscience. The basic foundational attitude is to let oneself be formed in the Church. Jesus wants men who are rooted and founded in the Church, men who:

> – seek their nourishment in the Word of God and do not allow themselves to be ensnared by political polarization or fashionable ideologies, which are ready to exploit their immense human potential;
>
> – avoid the ever present temptation of systematic protest and a hypercritical attitude, under the pretext of authenticity and a spirit of collaboration;
>
> – remain firmly attached to the local Church in which they are inserted, and to the universal Church, thus avoiding the very real danger of becoming isolated within themselves, then of believing themselves to be the only authentic Church of Christ, and hence of condemning the other ecclesial communities;
>
> – maintain a sincere communion with the pastors whom the Lord gives to his Church, and with the magisterium which the Spirit of Christ has entrusted to these pastors;
>
> – never look on themselves as the sole beneficiaries or sole agents of evangelization — or even the only depositaries of the Gospel — but, being aware that the Church is much more vast and diversified, accept the fact that this Church becomes incarnate in other ways than through themselves;
>
> – constantly grow in missionary consciousness, fervor, commitment, and zeal;
>
> – show themselves to be universal in all things and never sectarian. (*Evangelii nuntiandi*, 58)

The memory of our Fathers in the faith: defense against debilitating doctrines

The Lord who founds us evokes the image of the "ever greater Lord" *(Deus semper maior)* that Ignatius presents in the Principle and Foundation of the *Spiritual Exercises*. Let us meditate and pray today that we may let the Lord found us anew, and — at the same time — as pastors, that he may solidify the mission that we have been given: to found Christian hearts.

Let us remember all those zealous priests and bishops we have known and who now behold the Face of Christ (Pope John Paul II, *Pastores gregis*, 5). This memory will strengthen our heart and will defend us from being seduced *"by all kinds of strange teaching"* (Heb 13:9). We want to avoid doctrines that fail to found anything, but rather erode the solid foundations of a priestly heart. Such baseless doctrines also fail to nourish the faithful people of God. Let us listen to Dante, who offers some keen reflections on this timely topic:

> Christ did not say to his first company: "Go and preach idle stories to the world," but rather he gave them the foundation of truth; and this alone sounded on their lips, so that when fighting to ignite the faith, the Gospels served them as both shield and lance.[8]

---

8 *Non disse Cristo al primo suo convento:/ 'Andate e predicate al mondo ciance';/ ma diede lor verace fondamento;/ e quel tanto sonò ne le sue guance,/ sì ch'a pugnar per acceder la fede,/ de l'Evangelio fero scudo e lance.* (Paradiso 29, 109-114)

On the contrary, instead of furnishing a shield and lance, the seductive and divisive doctrines debilitate the hearts of the holy and faithful people of God, so that "the ignorant little sheep return from pasture having fed on wind."[9] When we need to renew our strength, let us call to mind the multitude of good pastors who have preceded us, and take the following exhortation from the Letter to the Hebrews to heart:

> *Therefore, since we are surrounded by so great a cloud of witnesses, let us rid ourselves of every burden and sin that clings to us and persevere in running the race that lies before us while keeping our eyes fixed on Jesus, the leader and perfecter of faith. For the sake of the joy that lay before him he endured the cross, despising its shame, and has taken his seat at the right of the throne of God. Consider how he endured such opposition from sinners, in order that you may not grow weary and lose heart. In your struggle against sin you have not yet resisted to the point of shedding blood.* (Heb 12:1-4)

The pastoral dimension of having Christ as our foundation

Jesus inaugurated the Kingdom of God. With his Word and his life he founded it in an irreversible manner: to belong to him is of inestimable value for us, and he founds us as pastors of his people. Such is his will for us. It is impossible to omit this *pastoral dimension* when we speak about the foundation of our lives.

---

9   .../ sì che le pecorelle, che non sanno,/ tornan del pasco pasciute di vento,/... (*Paradiso* 29, 106-107)

Like Mary, once we have been founded in the merciful love of the ever greater God, once fortified in our littleness by his loving gaze, once we have experienced his salvation and the great things he has done for us, we gain the courage to cast our gaze upon history, upon the people who have been entrusted to our care, to meet them with the hope-filled gaze of our Lady. As an aid to our meditation, let us turn to a pastoral document that truly calls us to let ourselves be founded anew, as pastors, by Christ our Lord.

I would like to propose several passages from the apostolic exhortation of Pope Paul VI, *Evangelii nuntiandi*.[10] In the light of this teaching, let us reflect on ourselves in order to draw some fruit. Jesus himself has a mission:

> Going from town to town, preaching to the poorest—
> and frequently the most receptive—the joyful news
> of the fulfillment of the promises and of the Covenant
> offered by God is the mission for which Jesus declares
> that he is sent by the Father. And all the aspects of his
> mystery—the Incarnation itself, his miracles, his teaching, the gathering together of the disciples, the sending
> out of the Twelve, the Cross and the resurrection, the
> permanence of his presence in the midst of his own—
> are components of his evangelizing activity. (*E.N.*, 6)

Through his evangelizing activity, Christ "first of all proclaims a kingdom, the kingdom of God; and this is so important that, by comparison, everything else becomes

---

10 All subsequent references to the apostolic exhortation *Evangelii nuntiandi* will be indicated by the abbreviation *E.N.* —Ed.

'the rest,' which is 'given in addition' [cf. Mt 6:33]. Only the kingdom therefore is absolute and it makes everything else relative" (*E.N.*, 8).

The Lord founds the Kingdom; we can continue this meditation by examining the different ways in which Jesus describes:

> – the happiness of belonging to this kingdom (a para-
> doxical happiness which is made up of things that the
> world rejects);
> – the demands of the kingdom and its Magna Charta;
> – the heralds of the kingdom, its mysteries, its children;
> – the vigilance and fidelity demanded of whoever
> awaits its definitive coming. (*E.N.*, 8)

The Lord founds us in his Kingdom, and his Spirit enables us feel the profound sense of belonging—a sense of belonging that coincides with the mystery of our very identity.

Jesus founds an evangelized and evangelizing community

Jesus founds a community that is simultaneously evangelized and evangelizing, since:

> Those who sincerely accept the Good News, through
> the power of this acceptance and of shared faith
> therefore gather together in Jesus' name in order
> to seek together the kingdom, build it up and live it.
> They make up a community which is in its turn evan-
> gelizing…. The Good News of the kingdom which
> is coming and which has begun is meant for all peo-
> ple of all times. Those who have received the Good
> News and who have been gathered by it into the

community of salvation can and must communicate and spread it. (*E.N.*,13)

The grace of our vocation: to evangelize

The task of evangelizing all people constitutes the essential mission of the Church. It is a task and mission which the vast and profound changes of present-day society make all the more urgent. *Evangelizing is in fact the grace and vocation proper to the Church, her deepest identity.* She exists in order to evangelize, that is to say, in order to preach and teach, to be the channel of the gift of grace, to reconcile sinners with God, and to perpetuate Christ's sacrifice in the Mass, which is the memorial of his Death and glorious Resurrection. (*E.N.*,14)

In our case, the grace of our vocation, our identity as an evangelizing community consists in letting ourselves be called together:

to proclaim with authority the Word of God, to assemble the scattered People of God, to feed this People with the signs of the action of Christ which are the sacraments, to set this People on the road to salvation, to maintain it in that unity of which we are, at different levels, active and living instruments, and unceasingly to keep this community gathered around Christ faithful to its deepest vocation. (*E.N.*, 68)

In founding Christian hearts, we are founded and rooted in Christ

Our mission, the very same one that frightens and makes us utter phrases like the ones mentioned earlier, is to evangelize and *shepherd the faithful people of God*. Let us repeat it once again: Jesus, in calling us for this mission, founds us in the deepest part of our heart; he founds us as pastors—this is our identity. In the exercise of our ministry, we are thus collaborating with Christ to found in turn, to found Christian hearts. Here is the amazing thing: at the same time as we go about this very same work, the Lord founds and roots our heart in his.

Piety as founding religious value: the fundamental hermeneutic of our theology

This community that Jesus founds:

> *objectively places man in relation with the plan of God*, with his living presence and with his action; she thus causes an encounter with the mystery of divine Paternity that bends over towards humanity. In other words, our religion effectively establishes with God an authentic and living relationship. (*E.N.*, 53)

What should not be lacking in our foundational task is the anointing[11] that is born from personal contact with the fidelity of the Lord of History. Our theology ought to be *pious* if it wants to be foundational, if it wants to live up to the claim that it was founded by the Lord. This piety must not serve as a sort of varnish applied to previous attitudes or ways of thinking. No, the piety I am talking about is, so to speak, *the fundamental hermeneutic of our theology*. It is life. When in our daily life we feel the presence

---

11   This key concept is developed at length in chapter 10, The Lord Who Anoints Us. —Ed.

of God, we have to say, "God is here." And when God is present, the first thing you do is get down on your knees.

It is only later that the human intellect tries to deepen our understanding and explain what it means that God is here. Thus we have the famous formula of Saint Anselm, "faith seeking understanding" *(fides quaerens intellectum)*, and the anecdotes about the saints studying theology on their knees. It is also worth highlighting another point that Pope Paul VI makes:

> Evangelization includes the preaching of the mystery of evil and of the active search for good. The preaching likewise — and this is always urgent — of the search for God himself through prayer which is principally that of adoration and thanksgiving, but also through communion with the visible sign of the encounter with God which is the Church of Jesus Christ; and this communion in its turn is expressed by the application of those other signs of Christ living and acting in the Church which are the sacraments." (*E.N.*, 28)

In sum, let us never forget that we are called to found and to let ourselves be founded by the Lord:

> In its totality, evangelization — over and above the preaching of a message — consists in the implantation of the Church, which does not exist without the driving force which is the sacramental life culminating in the Eucharist. (*E.N.*, 28)

III
The Lord Who Reprimands and Pardons Us

As we read the Gospels, a paradoxical pattern emerges: the Lord is more inclined to warn, correct, and reprimand those who are closest to him—his disciples and Peter in particular—than those who are distant. The Lord acts in this way to make it clear that ministry is a pure grace; it does not depend on the merits or competencies of the one chosen for the mission. In this context of the Lord's gratuitous choice and his absolute fidelity, to be reprimanded by him means that one is receiving a sign of God's immense mercy.

This is why we are now going to meditate on our sins from the perspective of our election by the Lord, focusing on our call to conversion and to follow him more closely. The Lord is the ever greater One: when he calls us to conversion, far from diminishing us, he is giving us stature in his Kingdom. From the hand of the Lord who corrects us also comes his abundant mercy.

The first confession of Simon Peter

I propose as the first point of meditation the passage in Luke about the vocation of the first disciples and what I call the first *confession* of Simon Peter (Lk 5:1-11). The scene unfolds within the context of evangelization. The Lord teaches the multitude from Peter's boat. Then he has his disciples put out into deep water, where he surprises them with the first miraculous catch. At the sight of this prodigy, Simon Peter confesses himself a sinner. And in this very act, the Lord converts him into a Fisher of men. Conversion and mission are thus intimately united in the heart of Simon Peter. The Lord accepts his *"Depart from me, Lord, for I am a sinful man"* (Lk 5:8), but he reorients it with his *"Do not be afraid; from now on you will be catching men"* (Lk 5:10).

From that moment on, Simon Peter never separates these two dimensions of his life: he will always confess that he is a sinful man and a fisher of men. His sins will not prevent him from accomplishing the mission he has received (and he will never become an isolated sinner enclosed within his own sinfulness). His mission will not allow him to hide his sin, concealed behind a pharisaical mask.

All of the new conversions Peter will undergo—through new corrections received from the Lord—all of them are founded upon the first grace he received at the Sea of Galilee. Thus, what follows from every sinner's conversion is mission: the desire that others may receive the same gift of forgiveness which Jesus has bestowed upon the pardoned sinner. True conversion always entails an apostolic dimension! It always means to stop focusing on one's "own interests" and to start looking after the "interests of Christ Jesus." The same is true for us bishops: we cannot receive a true mission, let alone carry it out effectively—evangelizing and guiding the people of God—without the profound awareness that we are pardoned sinners.

The Lord reprimands us for our dismissive tendencies, which stem from our lack of charity

In the miracle of the multiplication of loaves, the disciples offer the Lord some advice:

> *This is a deserted place and it is already very late. Dismiss them so that they can go to the surrounding farms and villages and buy themselves something to eat.* (Mk 6:35-36)

This seems like a reasonable suggestion, but the Lord responds in an unexpected way: *"Give them some food yourselves"* (Mk 6:37). This dismissive attitude is characteristic of the disciples and will be corrected again and again by the Lord. They also wanted Jesus to "get rid of" the Canaanite woman (Mt 15:23), and they "rebuked" those who brought their children to be blessed (Mk 10:13). On the other hand, the discussions among the disciples reveal that what really interested them was finding out who was the greatest…

With firmness and with patience the Lord corrects them. He is not in a hurry to dismiss the people nor is he bothered when they come close to him. The Lord does not put limits on the nearness of the people. He is the neighbor par excellence, the One who comes, God with us, the God who will be with us every day until the end of the world. The Lord is open to others, close to each one and to everyone. He lets himself be touched by the people who clamor for his presence, drawing from him grace after grace. This profound openness and availability reveals a total self-emptying that will find its most intense expression on the Cross, but which the Lord was living day after day.

Conversion from our sins, from our egoism, leads us to being available for others. The mission of a pastor is to "include" all the sheep (even those of "other flocks," as the Lord says [cf. Jn 10:16]). It implies a true conversion from our egoism, so that, in the moment of truth, we are well disposed to receive everyone, and not dismissive of anyone because of differences of character or narrowness of vision.

Perhaps at this point of the meditation it would be good, as pastors, to review what we see as problems and what we consider to be their solutions. How much room do we leave for the Lord? Do the solutions spring from faith and charity? Or do they come from a hands-off pastoral approach that amounts to saying: "Let them figure it out"? On the other hand, beware of the opposite approach: one that is so preoccupied with solving every problem right now that the Lord has no say in the matter. The work of the faithful servant turns into sterile activism!

The Lord reprimands us for the fears that arise from our lack of faith

In the Gospel passage where the Lord calms the storm, the disciples awaken him with a loud cry of complaint: *"Teacher, do you not care that we are perishing?"* After calming the storm, the Lord calms them with affectionate and instructive reproof: *"Why are you terrified? Do you not yet have faith?"* (Mk 4:35-41). Later he will calm them once again when they tire from rowing against the wind, and he comes toward them, walking on the water: *"Take courage, it is I; do not be afraid"* (Mk 6:50).

The Lord, in reprimanding them, links their fear with their lack of faith. He wants to persuade them that he is greater than every challenge, every trial, every temptation. And we are just like the Apostles in the storm! Dominated by fear, we too are more than capable of stumbling and falling into sin. For instance, there are pastors who do not accomplish their mission because they fear being labeled authoritarian. Others, afraid that the community entrusted to them might be made up of great sinners, commit the sin of not having mercy and hope. Others still, out of fear of being unable to lead the flock, try to rise above the difficult situation through, for example, an intellectual or mystical flight. Finally, there are others who, out of faintheartedness, fail to make firm decisions when they need to: things get brushed under the rug, dismissed and forgotten, only to return later in the form of horrifying scandals.

Fear makes us see ghosts, up to the point that sometimes the Lord himself appears to us and we imagine he is a ghost. Faith, on the other hand, gives us serenity and strength, fortifying us against impulsive and erratic reactions so characteristic of fear. The same goes for cowardice and temerity as well. Sometimes fear disguises itself as foolhardy bravery and we commit the sin of temerity, when evangelical reserve should be at work instead (cf. Mk 14:29, when the Lord corrects the temerity of Peter who claims that he will never deny him).

When Paul VI asked pastors to direct their evangelizing efforts to "the people of today," he dared to draw attention to what has become our habitual state of mind:

we are "are buoyed up by hope but at the same time often oppressed by fear and distress" (*E.N.*, 1). Hope and fear are intermingled even at the heart of our own apostolic life, above all in the decisions we make about how we work. We cannot risk making these decisions without having discerned what our fears and hopes are. For what is asked of us is nothing less than that "in this time of uncertainty and confusion, we may accomplish [our priestly ministry] with ever increasing love, zeal and joy" (*E.N.*, 1). And such a grace as this cannot be improvised.

For us, men of the Church, this discernment qualitatively transcends all the knowledge and know-how that the positive sciences have to offer, for it draws its power from an original vision, *the very originality of the Gospel*. The aim of these Spiritual Exercises is precisely to encounter this power of the Gospel anew. Thus we are gathered together today, consoled by one another's presence, *"mutually encouraged by our common faith"* (Rom 1:12). Such encouragement helps heal our apostolic hearts, so that we may recover both the coherence of our mission, our cohesion with the apostolic body, and the consonance between our thoughts, our feelings, and our actions.

We find ourselves here, sharing our faith, the faith of our Fathers, that is liberating in itself, in need of no addition or qualification. This faith justifies us before the Father who created us, before the Son who redeemed us and called us to follow him, before the Spirit who acts directly in our hearts. This faith—in the moment when we have to make concrete decisions—will lead us, under the anointing power of the Spirit:

– to a clear understanding of our limits;

– to be intelligent and wise stewards of the means at our disposal;

– and, finally, to evangelical efficacy, which is as far removed from navel-gazing ineptitude as it is from flight in the face of combat.

Our faith is revolutionary; it is a founding force in itself. Indeed, ours is a combative faith. While it surely does not pick fights, it does not flinch from pursuing a campaign under the discerning command of the Spirit, for the greater good of the Church. On the other hand, the liberating potential of our faith does not stem from ideologies but precisely from its contact with what is holy — faith is hierophany, "manifestation of the sacred." We think of the Virgin Mary who "intercedes," of the saints…

Our faith is so revolutionary that it is perpetually susceptible to the temptations of the enemy. Of course, it is not in the enemy's power to destroy it, but he can weaken the faith, make it dysfunctional, separate it from contact with the Most Holy, the Lord of all faith and all life. Then come the risks of falling into attitudes that, in theory, seem so distant from our own, but if we examine our apostolic activity we will see them hidden in our sinful heart. I would like to speak about these attitudes of convenience that allow us to exempt ourselves from difficult and demanding pastoral responsibilities. Let us look at some of these temptations.

One of the most serious temptations that deprives us of contact with the Lord is a defeatist attitude. When the enemy encounters faith, which is combative by definition, he disguises himself as an angel of light and starts sowing *seeds of pessimism*. No one engages in a battle unless he is fully convinced beforehand that he can win. The one who begins without confidence, has lost half the battle before it has begun. Christian triumph is always a cross, but a cross raised as a victory banner. Where can we acquire this invincible faith and be nourished by it? Among those who are humble. During these Spiritual Exercises we will remember many faces, the faces of the people entrusted to our pastoral care. The face of the humble ones, the face of those with simple piety, is always the face of triumph, and one that is almost always accompanied by a cross. Conversely, the face of the proud is always the face of defeat. He does accept the cross and wants a resurrection without having to pay the price. He separates what God has united.

The spirit of defeat tempts us to embark upon lost causes. The combative tenderness, for instance, that we behold in the seriousness of a child learning how to make the sign of the Cross, or in the profundity of an old woman saying her prayers, are absent in the spirit of defeat. Such is the faith, and such is the vaccine against the spirit of defeat (1 Jn 4:4; 5:4-5).

The Lord reprimands us for our weaknesses that come from our lack of hope

Suffering, which blossoms whenever one follows the will of God, is the essential condition of the Kingdom of God. On numerous occasions, the Lord brings this truth to the attention of his disciples, that they might take it to heart. Peter, for wanting to remove the Cross from the Gospel, is dubbed "Satan" by the Lord himself. Let us take the time to meditate upon the passage of Mk 8:31-33, in which the Lord firmly reprimands Peter and shows him that just as some thoughts are inspired by the Father, others "are not of God but of men."

It would be tempting to think that our mission as pastors could be accomplished without suffering. But it is precisely that, a temptation. Perhaps Saint Paul's expression "to support the community from below" (*hypomone*: patience, perseverance) represents the silent cross that all pastors must embrace. In any case, we need to understand that any other cross is a lure that prevents us from carrying our essential cross, the one that corresponds to our mission, namely, the weight of the community entrusted to our care. One does not invent the cross, nor does one take it up as if it were an unavoidable fate. It is the Lord who puts it on our shoulders and tells us: "Take up your cross and follow me." This cross is a yoke carried in tandem, and the Lord bears most of the weight.

In order to carry his cross the pastor will need the strength that comes from hope, which he should beg for in prayer. Then, for example, he will have the courage to make the necessary decisions, even if they are unpopular. He will also need magnanimity to begin difficult enterprises in service of God our Lord and to persevere in carrying them out without becoming discouraged when obstacles arise.

What is the criterion for discerning whether we are carrying the cross of our mission? When we no longer taste hope, that is a telltale sign. We then fall into a headlong search for extraordinary signs, even to the point of losing our memory, like the disciples of Emmaus, of the signs God has given us in the trials and difficulties of the Church throughout history. In the episode of Emmaus, we notice how the things the disciples "hoped for" were in contradiction with the Cross of the Lord. When he shows them that *"it was necessary that the Messiah should suffer these things in order to enter into the glory"* (Lk 24:26), their hearts begin to burn with true hope — hope that embraces the Cross.

The Lord reproaches us for our inability to keep watch with him

The bishop is the one who takes care of hope by keeping watch over his flock.

When Peter instructs his presbyters: *"God's flock is in your midst; give it a shepherd's care. Watch over it willingly as God would have you do, not under constraint; and not for shameful profit either, but generously"* (1 Pt 5:2), he enjoins them with a pastoral charge (*episkopountes*) that contains within it a variety of closely related spiritual attitudes: to supervise, to be vigilant, and *to keep watch*. In the back of Peter's mind as he offers these instructions undoubtedly lies the memory of the Lord's reproach on the night before the Passion: *"Simon, are you asleep?"* (Mk 14:37-38). The Lord wants us to keep watch with him.

This "keeping watch" can take on different shades of meaning. One is the spiritual attitude of bishop as supervisor (*epískopos* literally means "overseer"). Here the accent is placed on keeping an eye on the flock as a whole: the bishop attentively takes care to maintain its cohesion. Another spiritual attitude emphasizes vigilance, "watching out for" the flock: the *epískopos* is like a watchman, who sounds the alert when danger is imminent. Both of these attitudes are essential to the episcopal mission. However, they acquire full force when they dovetail with what I consider the most crucial attitude: *to keep watch*. One of the most evocative images of this attitude occurs in the Book of Exodus, where we are told that Yahweh kept a watch over his people during the night of Passover, also called "the night of vigil":

> *This was the night of vigil for the LORD, as he had led them out of the land of Egypt; so on this same night all the Israelites must keep a vigil for the LORD.* (Ex 12:42)

What I wish to underline here is the particular depth in what it means *to keep watch*, compared with supervision in the broader sense or watchful vigilance in a stricter sense. To supervise refers more to the concern for doctrine and ritual in their expression and practice, whereas *to keep watch* means making sure the people have enough salt and light in their hearts. To be vigilant means being on the lookout for danger, whereas *to keep watch* is more about patiently supporting the ways the Lord brings the salvation of his people to fruition. To be vigilant it is enough to be awake, alert, and shrewd. *To keep watch* requires meekness, patience, and the constancy of tested charity. To supervise means carefully inspecting the whole, without overlooking any details. *To keep watch* means knowing how to see the essentials. To supervise and to be vigilant both entail a certain degree of control. *To keep watch*, on the other hand, speaks of hope.

It is the hope of the merciful Father who keeps watch over the hearts of his growing sons. He lets them make their own way (of prodigality or accomplishment), ready to prepare a feast, so that, when they come back home, they encounter the embrace and loving dialogue that they need. This keeping watch in hope, which is the art of the *epískopos* (cf. Ps 63:7; 119:148), is expressed concretely in a prayer of blessing upon his children, spoken so beautifully by Moses to Aaron:

> *This is how you shall bless the Israelites. Say to them:*
> *"The LORD bless you and keep you!*
> *The LORD let his face to shine upon you, and be gracious to you!*
> *The LORD look upon you kindly, and give you peace!"*
> *So shall they invoke my name upon the Israelites, and I will bless them.* (Nm 6:24-27)

In this prayer—an "interpretation of hope" in itself—*to keep watch manifests and consolidates the "confidence" (parrhesia) of the bishop. Parrhesia consists in announcing the Gospel of Hope "so that the Cross of Christ might not be emptied of its meaning"* (1 Cor 1:17).

As we have just seen, two great images open and close the history of salvation, and in so doing embrace

it: the image of Yahweh who watches over the great exodus of the people of the Covenant and that of the merciful Father who watches and waits for his sons to return
home. Yet we have another image as well, even closer and
more familiar, but equally powerful: the figure of Saint
Joseph. In Joseph we encounter the faithful and fore-
sighted *epískopos* ordained by the Lord to serve as head
of his family. He is the man who watches over the Child
and his Mother, even in his dreams, and with the tenderness of a faithful and discreet servant, he lives out and
fulfills the Father's role. From this profound watchfulness
of Joseph springs that silent vision of the whole, capable of taking care of his little flock with meager means
(he transforms a manger for animals into the crib of the
Word incarnate!). From this watchfulness also comes the
vigilant and shrewd vision that succeeded in avoiding all
the dangers that threatened the Child.

Let us review all the times the Lord has reprimanded
us, and ask ourselves what he wishes to teach us through
them. And let us reflect on ourselves in order to make
amends. We should not be afraid of his reprimands, for
they are proof of the Lord's closeness to us, that he takes
us seriously. That he corrects us, just as he corrected
Peter, is a sign of our friendship with him and of our
apostolic zeal!

It will prove fruitful to conclude with a sincere dialogue with the Lord, our Lady, or God the Father, pon-
dering his patience and his magnanimity. He puts up with
us and corrects us and always helps us grow, without

ever belittling us or withdrawing his esteem and respect for us. Filled with contrition for our hardheadedness and our slowness to comprehend him, let us say like Peter, *"Lord, you know everything; you know that I love you."* While we offer our contrition, we feel the Lord encouraging us again, and he says to us: *"Feed my sheep"* (Jn 21:17).

IV
THE SPIRIT OF THE WORLD OR THE "ANTI-KINGDOM"

Do not love the world or the things in the world. If anyone loves the world, love for the Father is not in him. For all that is in the world, the lust of the flesh and the lust of the eyes and the pride of life, is not of the Father but is of the world. And the world passes away, and the lust of it; but he who does the will of God abides for ever. (1 Jn 2:15-17 RSV)

We know that we are of God, and the whole world is in the power of the Evil One. (1 Jn 5:19 RSV)

Just before the verses in the first passage above, the Apostle reminds us of our victory (cf. 1 Jn 2:12-14). It is like saying: "Do not fear the world," "We are sons of victors." Let us take the time to read these texts slowly, to draw strength from them. Even the tenderness contained in the expression: *"My little children"* (1 Jn 2:1, 12, 14, 18; 3:7, 18; 5:21) is a soft breath of strength to arm us in advance against the risk of becoming frightened when we enter into combat, or when we just think about it.

> *I have told you this so that you might have peace in me. In the world you will have trouble, but take courage, I have conquered the world.* (Jn 16:33)

What makes us believers and gives us the strength to battle against the world is precisely the memory of the salvation we have received. It is the hour of triumph and of the glorification of Jesus: *"The hour has come for the Son of man to be glorified.... Now is the time of judgment on this*

43

world; now the ruler of this world will be driven out" (Jn 12:23, 31). The Prince of this world has no power over Christ (Jn 14:30) because he is already judged (Jn 16:11).

Our memory of Christ's triumph brings this reality to life: our victory over the world is achieved through faith (1 Jn 5:4). Thus, we step into combat with valor. We advance "as victors," aiming to carry out Saint Paul's counsel: *"Be on your guard, stand firm in the faith, and act like men* [viriliter agite]. *In a word, be strong"* (1 Cor 16:13). We know that we can entrust all our worries to the Lord, since he always watches over us, even when the devil is prowling around us (cf. Pt 5:7-8).

Saint John exhorts us not to love the world, this world that seeks autonomy from God, this world that is an object of possession in every sense of the word. This world, which was created to lead us to God, has turned in upon itself, turning away from the Lordship of Christ, and thus turning into an evil "world." Such degradation is the daughter of lust: when "desire" turns into lust, then, indeed, we can speak of the "spirit of the world."

The spirit of the world

Jesus warns us against the spirit of the world. He defines it as the spirit that chokes the Word (Mt 13:22), like the father whose sons are much more cunning than the sons of light (Lk 16:8). This spirit of the world turns our lustful heart after the flesh, and our eyes toward prideful confidence in the things of this world (cf. 1 Tm 6:9; 1 Jn 2:16). The spirit of the world is the father of incredulity and of all impiety. It is precisely the god of this world that has blinded its heart (2 Cor 4:4), which is under the influence of a deceitful wisdom. It is unable to transcend the limits of its own egoism: *"Where is the debater of this age? Has not God made the wisdom of the world foolish?"* (1 Cor 1:20). *"Yet we do speak a wisdom to those who are mature, but not a wisdom of this age, nor of the rulers of this age who are passing away"* (1 Cor 2:6).

Saint Paul insists upon this counsel: *"Do not conform yourselves to this age"* (Rom 12:2). More literally: "Do not enter into the schemes of the world." This is the warning to us who were sinners and have known the Lord: *"You were dead in your transgressions and sins in which you once lived following the age of this world, following the ruler of the power of the air, the spirit that is now at work in the disobedient. All of us once lived among them in the desires of our flesh, following the wishes of the flesh and the impulses, and we were by nature children of wrath, like the rest"* (Eph 2:1-3). Thus it is that sin hardens our heart and makes us wicked.

Vanity

The spirit of this world aims to make us vain. This is a sickness of the heart so subtle that the Desert Fathers compare it to an onion. Why? Because, as they say, it is so difficult to get to its core: one peels away layer after layer but there's always something left. A vain heart is a safe haven for "ecclesiastical" forms of indiscipline and disobedience that disfigure the face of our holy Mother the Church. Look behind any episcopal posture of moralism, naïve optimism, or irenicism and you're sure to find a weak and vain heart, which—deep down—attempts to minimize the leadership responsibilities that have been entrusted to him by God.

These attitudes lead to the all too familiar fragmentation of the Church, resulting in a Gospel witness that is "rent by doctrinal disputes, ideological polarizations or mutual condemnations among Christians, at the mercy of the latter's differing views on Christ and the Church and even because of their different concepts of society and human institutions" (*E.N.*, 77). And it is these same postures, daughters of vanity, that uselessly give scandal to others, above all those who are weak in their faith, "with statements that may be clear for those who are already initiated but which for the faithful can be a source of bewilderment and scandal, like a wound in the soul" (*E.N.*, 79). Thus, our Mother the Church is torn apart from the inside...making a mockery of the "proof of credibility" that Christ entrusted to us: *"that all may be one...that the world may believe"* (Jn 17:21).

At the very heart of the Church—prototype until now of what is sacred and intangible, of what alone is truly solid and stable—we witness disrespect and criticism, division among Christians, the risk of secularism, the politicization of the Gospel, rampant disorientation, the loss of the very identity of the consecrated life, the danger of breaking the unity in doctrine and discipline. And all of this is done in the name of Jesus Christ and out of fidelity to his Gospel.[12]

---

12 Cardinal Eduardo Pironio, *Meditación para tiempos difíciles* (Ed. Patria Grande, Buenos Aires 2005), 2; [Eng., Meditation for Difficult Times, Boston:

The destabilization of the faithful and men and women of good will is clearly exacerbated when disunity is preached from the pulpits. We thus find Christians, priests, and religious who "come together in a spirit of bitter criticism of the Church, which they are quick to stigmatize as 'institutional' and to which they set themselves up in opposition as charismatic communities, free from structures and inspired only by the Gospel. Thus their obvious characteristic is an attitude of fault-finding and of rejection with regard to the Church's outward manifestations: her hierarchy, her signs. They are radically opposed to the Church. By following these lines their main inspiration very quickly becomes ideological, and it rarely happens that they do not quickly fall victim to some political option or current of thought, and then to a system, even a party, with all the attendant risks of becoming its instrument" (*E.N.*, 58). They end up questioning their membership in the Church, convinced that their own project takes precedence over that of our Mother the Church (cf. *E.N.*, 60). They decide to implant their own idea of the Church, but not "to implant the Church" (*E.N.*, 28).

Among the worldly sins against the truth of the Church, there exists today a kind of sinful zone into which we can easily fall. I am talking about forms of reductionism, whose objectives, means, and tactics are purely immanent, merely human. Already in his day, Paul VI drew our attention to this arena of combat and danger. We can benefit a great deal by meditating on what he says in numbers 32, 33, 35, 37, and 58 of *Evangelii nuntiandi*.

Daugheters of Saint Paul, 1977].

Hence, when preaching liberation and associating herself with those who are working and suffering for it, the Church is certainly not willing to restrict her mission only to the religious field and dissociate herself from man's temporal problems. Nevertheless she reaffirms the primacy of her spiritual vocation and refuses to replace the proclamation of the kingdom by the proclamation of forms of human liberation—she even states that her contribution to liberation is incomplete if she neglects to proclaim salvation in Jesus Christ. (*E.N.*, 34)

Perhaps it would do us good to suffer a bit before the Lord, asking pardon for the many times when, in our task as pastors, we have sinned in this area. The evil we may have done by falling into these naïveties is an evil that spreads. And if we find ourselves at fault, may the Lord lead us to sincere contrition and grant us the grace of a spirit of reparation and penance.

In the *Spiritual Exercises*, after having us meditate on sin in general and our own sins[13] in particular, Saint Ignatius invites us to make three spiritual conversations or colloquies:[14]

The first colloquy will be with our Blessed Lady, that she may obtain grace for me from her Son and Lord for three favors:

---

13 This takes place at the conclusion of the first week of the *Spiritual Exercises* where the retreatant has been guided to discover the mercy of God, which has made him a "pardoned sinner." —Ed.

14 This word simply means a "heart to heart" prayer, the prayer "of a friend to a friend." —Ed.

1. A deep knowledge of my sins and a feeling of abhorrence for them;

2. An understanding of the disorder of my actions, that filled with horror of them, I may amend my life and put it in order;

3. A knowledge of the world, that filled with horror, I may put away from me all that is worldly and vain. Then I will say a Hail Mary. (*Sp. Ex.*, 63)

Then he has us make the same three petitions to the Son and to the Father.

My attitude toward the world should be fundamentally the same as toward my own sins, toward the disordered and sinful roots in myself: keen awareness and aversion! From this attitude alone springs the desire for conversion. Which, in turn, over time, forges in us the faculty that is so solidly Christian: the capacity to judge. The "yes, yes... no, no"[15] that Jesus teaches us implies a spiritual maturity that rescues us from the superficiality of the foolish heart. A Christian needs to know what can be accepted and what must be condemned. We cannot sit down and "dialogue" with the enemy of our salvation: we need to meet him head on, ready to combat his every intention.

The liturgy has us address this petition to the Father: "Cleanse us from every stain of the old way of life" (Collect for Tuesday of the Third Week of Advent). Let us conclude the prayer with this petition, remembering that the grace we ask for is already assured by the Lord's own promise: *"I will remove from your midst the proud braggarts"* (Zep 3:11).

---

15 "Let your 'Yes' mean 'Yes,' and your 'No' mean 'No'" (Mt 5:37).

V
THE LORD WHO CALLS AND FORMS US

In the meditation on the Kingdom,[16] Saint Ignatius frames the contemplations on the life of Jesus within the context of a great call or vocation. The very life of the Lord is a call. His life says to us: "Come and follow me!" Its beauty beckons us, bidding us to follow after the Son in his ascent to the Father, a journey that passes by way of the Cross. Yes, the life of the Lord is a call! Our life, in response, will consist in following his lead, letting ourselves be formed by our Master—letting Jesus, gentle and humble of heart, fashion our hearts in the image of his own.

Following the Lord along the path of the Beatitudes

For us, following the Lord means obeying his commandments, as Saint John affirms: *"The way we may be sure that we know him is to keep his commandments.... Whoever claims to abide in him ought to live just as he lived"* (1 Jn 2:3,6). To keep the commandments, the Lord asks us to live the Beatitudes of the Kingdom, as a check against the illusion of close-fisted attitudes of generosity.

"Whoever says, 'I know him,' but does not keep his commandments is a liar, and the truth is not in him" (1 Jn 2:4). This is

---

16   The author alludes here to the second week of the *Spiritual Exercises*, which begins with the meditation on the Kingdom. This meditation opens with The Call of An Earthly King, which "will help us to contemplate the life of the eternal king" (*Sp. Ex.*, 91). The retreatant is thus called to make a qualitative leap from a humanitarian cause (service to a temporal king) to serving God and sharing in his life. —Ed.

the second lie, while the state of sin of the pagan soul is the first lie. To pretend that we know God without truly following him is the second lie. And we, pastors of the faithful people of God, we too can fall into this double life, this second lie.

In the Principle and Foundation of the *Spiritual Exercises* we ask for the grace to render justice to God, acknowledging him as Creator. Now we come face to face with our Savior. May we be granted the grace to do him justice by acknowledging him as such! What does it mean to do justice to the Savior? What does it mean to receive an overflowing measure of his saving justice? It means simply accepting the means that the Lord has chosen to save us: the way of the Beatitudes. In the Ignatian vision—realist with respect to spiritual combat—the Beatitudes are summed up in poverty and humiliations: "wrongs, abuse, and poverty," says Ignatius (*Sp. Ex.*, 98).

Following Christ in our pastoral work

In the reality of everyday life, humiliation and poverty take the form of work. It is the law of life that applies to everyone and makes us equal to one another. However, we are not readily inclined to want to rejoice or suffer with or like others. Thus, in order to remain faithful in the service of the Kingdom, we must make an effort to embrace what is, in the eyes of an egoist, humility and poverty.

To follow Christ closely means we want to go farther. It means following him on the road he traveled first, living as he lived:

It is my will is to conquer all the lands of the infidel. Therefore, whoever wishes to join with me in this enterprise must be content with the same food, drink, clothing, etc. as mine. So, too, he must work with me by day, and watch with me by night, etc., that as he has had a share in the toil with me, afterwards he may share in the victory with me.[17] (*Sp. Ex.*, 93).

To follow Christ closely means we do all this out of love, conscious that apart from him we can do nothing (Jn 15:1-5). We do all this without setting conditions on his call (Lk 9:23-26; 9:57-62). We do it all firmly convinced that the Son of Man has nowhere to lay his head, that death does not stop life, and that whoever starts to look back with longing upon the "garlic and onions of Egypt" (cf. Nm 11:5) is not fit for the Kingdom.

The style of apostolic work: I want, I desire, and it is my deliberate choice

To follow Jesus who invites us to enter into the Kingdom means to follow him in our pastoral work. We shall conclude this meditation offering our very selves to this work, and we will do so with the words Ignatius uses to convey the character of apostolic work: "I want and I desire and it is my deliberate choice"[18] (*Sp. Ex.*, 98).

"I want" is opposed to velleity;[19] "desire" is opposed

---

17   This is the call of the "earthly king." It is worth noting the repeated use of "with" and "as": "With him in toil, with him in joy!" —Ed.
18   These words are part of the offering that the retreatant makes at the end of the meditation on the Kingdom. —Ed.
19   Velleity is the lowest form of volition: a wish or inclination not strong enough to lead to action. —Ed.

acedia;[20] and "deliberate choice" is opposed to inconstancy. This resolute affirmation of Saint Ignatius runs counter to all fickle and fleeting desires that are no more than veiled forms of inconstancy and symptoms of spiritual acedia.

To do justice to the faithful people of God means being completely dedicated to leading one's flock, in responding to their sometimes tiring requests to be touched by God at any time: sacraments, blessings, words.... The holy people of God tire their pastor out because they ask for concrete things. However, it is easy to let ourselves be seduced by work that allows us to retreat into an imaginary realm. Within our minds we are kings and lords, and if we spend too much time cultivating our imagination, then we will never feel the urgency of the concrete. The pastoral work of our dioceses and parishes is altogether different. Certainly, it requires reflection and intellectual work, but fundamentally, the majority of our time is devoted to works of charity.

Charity is absolutely necessary in order to respond with the same enthusiasm to the people who come asking for the widest variety of things: one asks if it is possible to back out of a commitment, another asks for a baptismal certificate in the cathedral, another asks for a requiem Mass on one day and not another. People are demanding when it comes to matters of religion! It is normal that one who is faithful in carrying out his or her Christian duties to one's family and to society should expect

---

20   Acedia is a state of spiritual torpor characterized by discouragement, boredom, sloth, and distaste for prayer. —Ed.

the same level of fidelity in pastoral attention from those who have been charged with the task of giving it. The priest and the bishop do not belong to themselves. From time to time they can find refuge in "other things," but all these "other things" quickly fall away in the presence of a mother of a family who makes them walk blocks or drive miles to bless a house.

We have to do justice to the faithful people of God.

The apostolic constancy that creates institutions

Apostolic constancy is founded upon a firmly determined will. What is more, when the will in a group is strong, then an institution develops. And, as we know, nothing works well between human beings without institutions. The true government is the one that legislates, that leaves a legacy of laws to its people so that they can govern themselves in the future. The Church is visible; it is not simply spiritual, pneumatic. The visible Church means a visible organization that all can see. A pastoral institution has a body and a soul, it has a tradition and a charism, it has a history and a present. We could be all alone on a mission, but the Church would be right there. Each member of the body reproduces in himself the whole institution in its totality. The Church always seeks living institutions, where the Spirit is at work, because a dead tradition is worth nothing. The Church is not called to be a merely formal organization, based on bureaucratic paperwork or the idolatry of numbers. We need the law, but it is the Spirit who gives life. This does not mean, of course, that the Church can leave things to the inspiration of the moment.

What is the source of ecclesial institutions — missions, parishes, religious orders? There is only one, one alone, dear to the heart of Christ our Lord. Like all things of the Lord, it is given in secret and grows like the seed carefully tended by the hand of God. The one and only source of the visible institutions of the Church are the sacraments, born from the open side of Christ — among them, the Eucharist and baptism. At times one hears talk of sacramentalism versus evangelization, as if they were competing realities (*E.N.*, 47). What has been forgotten, however, is this: in the administration of the sacraments, with the solid support of a global catechism, a hidden organization pulses within the heart of the faithful. What does a pastoral institution aim for if not the perfection of the grace of baptism, in order to extend the Kingdom of Christ? And what is the aim of a mission, a diocese, or a parish? Is it not to support and strengthen life itself? And how does this come about if not through a fully sacramental institution, whose "admirable fecundity of grace and holiness are the living expression of the supernatural life" (*E.N.*, 47)? This is the bedrock of our apostolic constancy and the creative wellspring of our institutional life. It seems to me that the hands of a missionary, a parish priest, a bishop, more than merely going through the routine motions of a ritual, should rather tremble with emotion when they administer the sacraments, because these gestures effectively forge the foundations of institutions.

Apostolic faithfulness is one of the institutional dimensions of the Church, and we have to fortify it against the vice of acedia with our constant work, and the work of our constancy. Why? Because it is the fruit of the promise we make today before the Lord: "I want and I desire and it is my deliberate choice." Let us pause a moment now to ponder this anti-apostolic vice of acedia, which eats away at our mission as pastors of the faithful people of God.

Acedia

Every form of acedia functions like a utopia: a kind of careless disregard for the "persons, places, and times" that are concretely involved in our pastoral activity. A philosopher might say that such a person pretends to operate outside of space and time. Acedia can take on various guises in our life as pastors, so we need to remain alert in order to discern how it camouflages itself. At times it appears as paralysis, when one can no longer accept the rhythm of life. At other times, it is the hyperactive pastor whose giddy comings and goings reveal an inability to ground himself in God and in his concrete circumstances. On other occasions, acedia manifests itself in ambitious plans hatched without any attention to the nitty gritty involved in getting such a project off the ground, let alone sustaining it. Conversely, it can take the form of getting tied up in knots about immediate details, unable to integrate them within the larger vision of God's plan. In this context, the epitaph of Saint Ignatius is instructive: "Not to be confined by the greatest, yet to be contained within the smallest, is divine" (*Non coerceri a maximo, contineri tamen a minimo, divinum est*). It is important to recognize that acedia is a divisive and debilitating force; what unites is life, and those under the sway of acedia are deprived of life.

We need to admit that acedia visits us frequently, and to view it as a very real threat to our daily life as pastors. Humbly acknowledging that it exists in us should move us to seek nourishment in the Word of God that gives us the strength to want, to desire, and to choose deliberately—in full freedom. For we know that the "new commandment" calls for *total* engagement.

At the outset of the meditation of the Kingdom of Christ, Saint Ignatius invites the retreatant to make a "compostion of place": "Here it will be to see in imagination the synagogues, villages, and towns where Christ our Lord preached" (*Sp. Ex.*, 91). Announcing the Gospel demands apostolic constancy, a daily determination to say, "I want, *I desire*, and it is my deliberate choice" (*Sp. Ex.*, 98). Without letting up. It is not enough to say, like the rich young man, *"All of these I have observed from my youth"* (Mk 10:20). The "Come and follow me" is like that of Peter, who hears the call—and leaves everything (Lk 18:28-30).

Pouring oneself out, day after day, in pastoral service

Only a worker who has discovered how to break free from triviality, acedia, and inconstancy, in order to *pour himself out all day and every day in pastoral service*—only a pastor such as this can understand in his heart the cost of Christ's redemption. His worker's hands protect and nurture the unity of the Church, making it grow. This participation in the work of God, born of belonging to Holy Mother Church, makes us sons of the Father, brothers among brothers, and fathers of the faithful people of God. Only the tireless worker knows, in his "I want and I desire and it is my deliberate choice," how to preserve the "immaculate unity" of the Church, as saint Ignatius of Antioch calls it (Letter to the Ephesians, 4.2).

Just as our sin acquires its true gravity in the presence of Christ, so does the law acquire its true grandeur when we follow the Lord. One can begin to follow him out of mere curiosity: *"Rabbi, where are you staying?"* (Jn 1:35-51). If one stays with him, however, it always leads in the end to the most absolute self-surrender: *"As a young man you fastened your belt and went about as you pleased; but when you are older you will stretch out your hands, and another will tie you fast and carry you off against your will"* (Jn 21:18). We can only follow Jesus in everyday toil and fatigue, with its crosses and agonies (Mk 14:33), with its joys and consolations (Mk 9:2), keeping our gaze ever fixed upon the Lord:

> *Looking to Jesus the pioneer and perfecter of our faith, who for the joy that was set before him endured the Cross, despising the shame, and is seated at the right hand of the throne of God.* (Heb 12:2 RSV)

We conclude our prayer by making the *offering of ourselves to work*. All the heavenly court is present. My oblation is made public before the Church Triumphant, for the salvation of the faithful people of God.

Eternal Lord of all things, in the presence of Thy infinite goodness, and of Thy glorious mother, and of all the saints of Thy heavenly court, this is the offering of myself which I make with Thy favor and help. I protest that it is my earnest desire and my deliberate choice, provided only it is for Thy greater service and praise, to imitate Thee in bearing all wrongs and all abuse and all poverty, both actual and spiritual, should Thy most holy majesty deign to choose and admit me to such a state and way of life.[21] (*Sp. Ex.*, 98)

---

21 The author cites here the prayer of Offering that closes the meditation on the Kingdom.

VI

The Lord Who Forms Us

Between the first and second week of the *Spiritual Exercises*, that is, just before the meditation on the Kingdom, Saint Ignatius inserts some Additions (additional directions) "to help one go through the exercises better and find more readily what he desires" (*Sp. Ex.*, 73-90). Then the second week begins, opening with the contemplations on the hidden life of Christ. In the course of these contemplative exercises, we ask for "an intimate knowledge of our Lord, who has become man for me, that I may love him more and follow him more closely." (*Sp. Ex.*, 104). The dynamic of this structure [Additions — Kingdom — Hidden Life] is incarnational and formative: Christ takes form in us (cf. Gal 4:19) through interior bonds of friendship. We have already seen signs of this friendship in the meditation on the Kingdom:

> Whoever wishes to join me in this enterprise must be willing to labor with me, that by following me in suffering, he may follow me in glory. (*Sp. Ex.*, 95)

Nazareth is a permanent dimension of the apostolic man

We should not consider the hidden life of Jesus as a preparatory stage to the public life. Rather, it is the very synthesis of the whole life of the Lord. Sometimes we think of the hidden life of Christ as analogous to our time in formation for the priesthood, and of his public life as analogous to the years following our ordination. But it is not like this at all, because *Nazareth is a permanent dimension of the apostolic man.* Whoever wants more action needs more contemplation. Whoever has to make more decisions in Christ is in need of more formation in Christ. Nazareth is like the touchstone for testing the depth of our apostolate.

This is why we can speak of Nazareth as the hidden force that makes our apostolate an authentic force of institutionalization of the work of the Kingdom. Nazareth makes us body and member of a Body. The hidden life enables us to shoot straight and hit the target, instead of shooting in the dark. It sets us to work cementing the foundations of history, rather than working "part-time" in apostolates without roots.

Growth of the Word in us as permanent formation

Saint Luke insists on the mystery that *"the Child grew"* (Lk 2:40), and he affirms this mystery again in the Acts of the Apostles: *"the Word continued to spread and grow"* (Acts 12:24; 19:20). We who began our apostolic journey years ago, are we still inhabited by the hope that filled our sails in the beginning? Are we convinced that the Word can still grow stronger and deeper within us? Do we still believe that the Lord has many more spiritual treasures to reveal to us in contemplation? Do we still have the fervent desire to grow day after day in service to the Lord? For example, by continually educating and renewing ourselves through a program of permanent formation?

The hidden life as the place of first love

We know from experience that, at this stage in our lives, temptations are no less numerous, and that our original ideals have a tendency to wane: *"Yet I hold this against you: you have lost the love you had at first"* (Rv 2:4). Similarly, our memory of the "great things the Lord has done" might get a little hazy. We are conscious of the combat that we must engage in to remain loyal in our service to Christ and in our belonging to his Church. Precisely for these reasons, contemplation of the hidden life is the place where we rediscover our first love, where we come in contact again with the source of salvation, with the love of Mary who conceived the Word, the love of Mary and of Joseph who take care of him and form him in Bethlehem, in Nazareth, and in Egypt. What better way to replenish our soul than to become a simple disciple again, to become a little child who needs to be cared for and formed anew, especially for one whose constant task is to be teacher, pastor, judge, and head! Let us draw close to the Lord, in whose presence we are always disciples, always children.

The hidden life renews our hope calming all discouragement and anxiety

When contemplative fervor for the hidden life grows cold, when the fire for formation smolders, we feel discouragement and disenchantment pass close by—when they don't nest in our hearts—discouragement and disenchantment as if everything was already old, finished. Then we are overcome by inertia, or the opposite, anxiety to do all things over again as if they were new, as if they had no history, without memory. This is when the conflicts characteristic of our times can undermine our *hope*, evacuating it of meaning, reducing it to a slogan.

The hidden life restores the warmth of charity tempering all activism

At other times, in an effort to respond to the problems of today's world, we channel our apostolic energies into various forms of activism, even purely secular ones. Throwing ourselves into this activity, it's as if the value of our charity as men of the Church could be measured according to how much time we dedicate to action, or how many apostolic organizations we foster and promote. This amounts to a truncated apostolate, cut off from the *maternal warmth of the Church*.

The hidden life fortifies our faith pacifying all possessive anxiety

Finally, our nature as men, born to be fruitful, moves us from within and can lead us to take possession of all those whom we help to grow in Christ, to want to make them ours. It is as if we want to possess the flock rather than shepherd it: our surreptitious aim is that our faithful belong more to us than to the Church. Our faith as pastors then becomes possessive, controlling, and mistrustful.

All these temptations, and others, are familiar to us; we can all recall concrete instances from our own experience. They limit our growth in the Lord and narrow our horizons, reducing our vision to the dimensions of our consciousness.

And so here we are, with our daily lives, our loyalties and our sins, our hopes and our temptations. We must approach the crib of Jesus with the desire to be touched by his grace, that it will help us continue to grow in his service. And like "unworthy little slaves," as Ignatius says, we renew *our hope* by contemplating that a Child has been given to us in the middle of the human family, old with age. Our *apostolic charity* will draw strength before the maternal warmth and fecundity of the Virgin. And we can also turn our gaze toward Saint Joseph, the man who assumed paternal charge of the Child he did not sire. He inspires us to an ever greater *faith* in our own specific religious paternity.

Meditation with Saint Joseph

The "ever greater God" who is always greater and invites us to follow him is a Lord who takes us seriously, takes up our weakness, our pusillanimity. It will do us good to listen to the Lord's *"Do not be afraid!"* When he says to us, *"Do not be afraid!"* it is as if to say, *"Have confidence!"* This word reaches our hearts and saves us.

In the infancy narratives, God often tells Joseph and Mary: *"Do not be afraid." "The angel of the Lord appeared in a dream and said to him, 'Joseph, son of David, have no fear about taking Mary as your wife. It is by the Holy Spirit that she has conceived this child'* (Mt 1:20). Do not be afraid to recognize him, to bring him into the lineage of David, because he comes from the Holy Spirit and will save his people. In essence, the angel tells him, "Do not lack confidence in Mary." In another dream, the angel warns him to fear for the life of the Child and to protect this life, adding that he should fear Herod and flee (Mt 2:13-15). Here fear means "to look after." It is as if we hear: Do not be afraid to take upon yourself whatever task is necessary to protect this life, to save this Child. Joseph will later receive the order to return, and as the Evangelist notes, upon returning and learning that the son of Herod was king in Judea, Joseph *"was afraid"* (Mt 2:22). Then, having received confirmation in a dream, he changed his route.

What is said about Joseph can be summarized like this: accept the mission from God, let yourself be led by God, embrace the hardship and danger in order to save the Savior. Joseph saves Mary's reputation, the lineage of Jesus, the integrity of the Child, his rootedness in the land of Israel.... But at the same time he the first one saved by God from a false conception of justice, closed God's designs. Joseph is also saved from an isolated life, from a life that would have been perhaps less turbulent, but that would have lacked the the consolation of carrying God in his arms.

Rereading chapter 11 of the Letter to the Hebrews with the eyes and the heart of Joseph, let us ponder the Lord's powerful refrain of "Do not be afraid":

– Do not be afraid to pass beyond what is visible toward the invisible.

– Do not be afraid of Cain, for though dead, you will speak.

– Do not be afraid to come close to God, because he exists and rewards those who seek him.

– Do not be afraid to save your family and condemn the world.

– Do not be afraid to hope to live in that city whose architect and builder is God.

– Do not be not afraid to be subjected to the test, even if it costs you your first born.

– Do not be afraid to believe that by the power of God the walls of the enemy will fall.

Behind this *"Do not be afraid!"* stands the "Do not be afraid to take up your cross and follow me." And paradoxically there is also one fear that we should jealously guard: *"Therefore, let us be on our guard while the promise of entering into his rest remains, that none of you seem to have failed"* (Heb 4:1).

The Lord's *"Do not be afraid!"* becomes a "Take courage!" With the Letter to the Hebrews and its symbols we can express this *"Take courage!"* as follows:

– Have the courage to conquer the Fatherland, even if it entails personal sacrifice.

– Have the courage to build the City, even if it means abandoning our preconceived ideas about it.

– We rejoice in letting God's scalpel fashion us a face, even if it effaces certain grins we were fond of.

The courage we have in mind here is the courage to receive the power of God, which is *parrhesia* (bold assurance) and joyful humor; it is the sage simplicity that will teach us, like Joseph, to "welcome the Promise from afar."[22]

---

22 A reference to Abraham, "who knew how to welcome the promises from afar and to rejoice in the prospect of the Day of Jesus" (cf. Jn 8:56). Joseph had a similar experience of the "Day" of Jesus, in that he died before the public life, Passion, Death, and glorious Resurrection of the Savior. —Ed.

VII

The Lord Who Battles for and with Us

The contemplation of the mysteries of the public life of the Lord begins with the meditation on the Two Standards.[23] It is a meditation that takes the form of a plan — a battle plan.

The Lord sends us into spiritual combat. It is a fight to the death that he himself has undertaken, and one that we too are invited to identify as our own ultimate battleground, conscious that it is God's war. For it is a war waged "against the enemy of human nature" (*Sp. Ex.*, 136), that is, in the language of Saint Ignatius, the Devil or Demon. It is also the war waged by "the friend of human nature," the Lord Jesus, who wants to win us for God and to recapitulate in himself all that is good in creation, in order to offer it to the Father, to the praise of his glory.

What is at stake in this war? It is whether in my heart, as well as in the heart of the Church and of humanity itself, the Kingdom of heaven will be established, with its law of love and the Lord's way of life: poverty, humility, and service. Or whether the kingdom of this world will triumph, with its laws and values of wealth, vanity, and pride.

It is characteristic of Ignatius to have us contemplate the mysteries of the life of the Lord while at the same time inviting us "to investigate and ask in what kind of life or in what kind of state his Divine Majesty wishes to make

---

23   We have already alluded to this meditation in note 3. —Ed.

use of us (*Sp. Ex.*, 135). And if we have already chosen a state of life, we should reform it for the better. This is not a question of fulfilling one's responsibilities or "positions of service" but of something deeper and definitive: it is a matter of my *state of life*. And this should not be understood as an external form but as a vital principle: In what state of life, or with what reform to my state of life, will my heart become *more* a "friend of Jesus"? How can I become more like him, more poor, more humble, and more dedicated to service? In what state of life, or through what reform to my state of life, will the love of Jesus take definitive root in me?

The objective context in which we can pose this question is the life and death battle between the Two Standards. Cardinal Martini[24] speaks of "two opposing life projects" (life and death, progress or degradation of human existence). Two battle plans with no room for a no-man's-land of "more or less." Only the law of contraries applies: either one or the other.

We often conceive of pastoral situations as linear or developmental: from bad to good, from good to better; or as regressive: from good to less good, and then to bad. And we complain when good development does not take place or when it is slow. As a result, we take bitter note of the weakening of the faith, declining Mass attendance...and we compare today with the good old days. We run the risk of turning something that is in flux into something static.

---

24   Cardinal Carlo Maria Martini, *Mettere ordine nella propria vita* (Piemme, 1992), 111 [Eng., *Letting God Free Us: Meditations on Ignatian Spiritual Exercises*, trans. Richard Arnandez (New City Press, 1994)].

We forget that the Christian life is a continual battle against the seductive power of idols, against Satan and his effort to lead man to unbelief, to despair, to moral and physical suicide. We forget that the Christian road is measured not only by the distance traveled, but also *by the magnitude of the battle, by the difficulties encountered, by the obstacles overcome, and by the ferocity of the assaults that have been repulsed.*

This is why arriving at a sober assessment of the faith in our day is so complicated. Sociological statistics are not sufficient. It is not enough to count the number of Christians, the number who practice, etc. One also has to consider the sometimes dramatic battles that Christians must wage every day in order to continue believing and acting according to the Gospel.

The meditation on the Two Standards teaches us that the Lord sees us as his people engaged in a battle against the enemy, and he is full of compassion. He gives us courage, he sustains and consoles us. The Lord is the great Commander-in-Chief who rallies his troops and leads them into battle. He continually reinvigorates and comforts each and every one of us, because he knows the battle is hard, and the Evil One is cunning and ruthless.

Nevertheless, fighting shoulder to shoulder with the Lord is a source of constant joy. And this joy enables us to overcome the numerous frustrations that inevitably arise, for example, with a business model of pastoral "management." We should ask the Lord for the grace to cherish this dramatic sense of Christian life. While the way we have been describing it may be hard for some to appreciate, in the heat of battle it produces fruits of joy and peace. More "peaceful" or conciliatory language might sound pleasant to the ear, but in practice it provides little consolation.

Spiritual discernment

Beloved, do not trust every spirit, but put the spirits to a test to see if they belong to God, because many false prophets have appeared in the world.... You are of God, litte ones, and thus you have conquered the false prophets. For there is One greater in you than there is in the world. (1 John 4:1, 4)

This warning of Saint John is an invitation to sagacity, to keen and farsighted judgment. In the battle for the Kingdom, we cannot afford the luxury of being naïve. This sagacity leads to wisdom and operates with discernment, which is not a simple exercise of one's own spirit. In a heart disposed by the active presence of the Holy Spirit, discernment is the capacity to recognize the work of God and the temptations of the Demon. Discernment is possible only by being open to the action of God. The superficial spirit, full of one's self, is incapable of this: such a one lets himself be lured by the appearance of truth that cloaks all prophets of deceit and vainglory.

Discernment also does not consist in attending to the back and forth of one's interior reactions, as if they were autonomous.

All "movement of spirits" has an origin:

I presuppose that there are three kinds of thoughts in my mind, namely: one which is strictly my own, and arises wholly from my own free will; two others which come from without, the one from the good spirit, and the other from the evil one. (*Sp. Ex.*, 32)

To discern between these thoughts, we must discover their origin and their direction, in order not to be fooled by the evil spirit and to follow the inspirations of the Lord at all times. Finally, discernment cannot be done from an antiseptic standpoint, as if we were spectators of a battle that did not involve us. We exercise discernment by fundamentally adhering to the Lord with this desire as our goal: "the conquest of self and the regulation of one's life in such a way that no decision is made under the influence of any inordinate attachment"[25] (*Sp. Ex.*, 21).

From here Saint John announces a criterion for discernment: the confession of the scandal of the Incarnation, the proclamation of Jesus Christ, the Word of God come in the flesh.

> *This is how you can recognize God's Spirit: every spirit that acknowledges Jesus Christ come in the flesh belongs to God, while every spirit that fails to acknowledge him does not belong to God. Such is the spirit of the antichrist which, as you have heard, is to come; in fact, it is in the world already.* (1 Jn 4:2-3)

The evil spirit always divides, and divides Jesus. Thus it denies unity. Divisions that call Christ and his Church into question are signs of the presence of antichrists and of the Demon. All forms of division, of Manichaeism, reenact the sin of the first angels (one theological tradition

---

25   This is how Saint Ignatius defines the *Spiritual Exercises*. —Ed.

attributes the sin of the angels to their opposition to the project of the Incarnation). Conversely, to confess that the Word of God has come in the flesh — *indivise et inconfuse* (without division or confusion), as the Chalcedonian formula puts it — is from the Spirit of God. This draws our attention to the fact that throughout the history of the Church, all deviation from this understanding has had a strong impact upon the Body of the Lord: whether it be on the subject of the Eucharist, or of the poor (who are the suffering body of Christ), or of the Church as Body, particularly with regard to her union with the Lord as Head.

We put our discernment into practice by founding ourselves upon faith in the Word of God made flesh, born of the Blessed Virgin Mary through the work of the Holy Spirit, who suffered and died under Pontius Pilate, and who rose again on the third day. We discern by founding ourselves upon faith in Christ, true God and true man, whose human nature is without division or confusion (*indivise et inconfuse*), united to his divinity.

Intimate knowledge of the snares of the Devil

Saint Ignatius underscores the need for wisdom and sagacity:

> Ask for a knowledge of the deceits of the rebel chief and help to guard myself against them; and also ask for a knowledge of the true life exemplified in the sovereign and true Commander, and the grace to imitate him. (*Sp. Ex.*, 139)

Knowledge of "the true life" consists in placing ourselves under the Standard of Christ, enlisting in his service to follow him into battle — as victors (1 Jn 2:4-20). We constantly renew our faith in the knowledge that this Standard is a victory banner. Indeed, in combating the appearance and vanity of the Evil One's pseudo-truths, we must remain on our guard at all times, lest we be deceived by an "angel of light" in disguise (2 Cor 11:14). Then we would know the cruelest defeat of all: to have started to serve under the Standard of Christ, and then, little by little, to let oneself slip behind enemy lines — for good. This is the defeat of having abandoned your "first love" (cf. Rv 2:4; Jer 2:2). It is the worst temptation, especially for us bishops: once installed as chief steward of the house, one starts beating the servants! *"And the last state of that man is worse than the first"* (Lk 11:26).

Riches, vainglory, and pride

In his campaign to make us fall, the Demon always uses the same tactical approach: riches, vainglory, and pride. From here issue all the other sins and vices.

> Consider the address he makes to them, how he goads them on to lay snares for men and bind them with chains. First they are to tempt them to covet riches (as Satan himself is accustomed to do in most cases) that they may the more easily attain the empty honors of this world, then come to overweening pride. The first step, then, will be riches, the second honor, the third pride. From these three steps the evil one leads to all other vices. (*Sp. Ex.*, 142)

This demonic strategy was already at work in the temptations of Jesus in the desert (Lk 4:3-12), and is reflected across the entire Christian tradition.[26]

Discernment of idolatries and intimate knowledge of the Lord

In order to follow the Lord ever more closely, we must be ever ready to wage war. Discernment is the essential weapon for this kind of warfare. We cannot trust any and every spirit. We must look to see if it comes from God. This is why there is an intimate connection between following the Lord and the knowledge that we have of him. The better we know him, the better we recognize the sound of his voice. At first, we come to know him by a certain *connaturality*, which is nothing other than the presence of the Holy Spirit moving our "restless hearts" to seek our rest in him. And as we persevere along this path, we discover that the Lord unveils his Heart and his mystery more and more to us. This is why, in guiding our flock to know and serve God more faithfully, we must insist more upon the *dispositions of heart* than upon the work of the intellect: "Our intention must be simple. I must consider only the end for which I am created" (*Sp. Ex.*, 169).

Only a transparent heart sees God (Lk 11:34-36; Mt 5:8).

---

26   Cf. Saint Thomas Aquinas, *S.Th.*, I-II, q.84, a.1 co: *Cupiditas...dicitur radix omnium peccatorum.... Videmus enim quod per divitias homo acquirit facultatem perpetrandi quodcumque peccatum.* (Covetousness...is called the root of all sins.... For we see that by riches man acquires the means of committing any sin whatever.)

The temptation to idolatry

As we follow the path of the Lord, there is always the risk, to a greater or lesser extent, of letting our guard down and abandoning vigilance. If and when this occurs, it is usually a sign that one has succumbed to a masked temptation to idolatry. This consists in reducing the Lord's gifts — or the Lord himself! — to an object that we fit into our own egoistic categories. In so doing, we fabricate an idol, which is essentially impotent and ultimately ineffective. Yet this idol becomes the locus of our hope. A heart that is vigilant, on the other hand, one that is receptive to the wisdom of the Holy Spirit and imbued with sagacity, is instantly suspicious of any tendency to instrumentalize God, whether for blatantly selfish reasons or for putatively pastoral ones. In order to fend off such temptations, the sagacious heart humbly opens itself before the Word of God, that it may destroy the idols that impede him from following Christ and try to distort his knowledge of the Lord:

> *"You have lost the love you had at first."* (Rv 2:4)
> *"There are some among you who follow the teaching of Balaam."* (Rv 2:14)
> *"You tolerate Jezebel — that self-styled prophetess who seduces my servants."* (Rv 2:20)
> *"You are dead. ..... I find that the sum of your deeds is less than complete in the sight of my God." (Rv 3:12)*
> *"You are lukewarm."* (Rv 3:16)

When we discover that our heart is in possession of such idols, which are like veritable teraphim[27] because of

---

27   This word, which means "images" or "likenesses," is used in connection

the tender affection we hold for them, we should listen attentively to the prophetic denunciations against idolatry pronounced by Isaiah and Jeremiah (Is 40:18-20; 43:10-13; 44:9-10; Jer 10:1-9). Let us always remember that Jesus has conquered every possible temptation, including the temptation to appropriate God's gifts for ourselves, instrumentalizing them as means to our self-serving ends.

Following close behind the banner of Jesus will reveal many things hidden in our heart

Casting down the idols that can crop up even as we follow the Lord means to accept that Christ is a sign of contradiction. The generous believer is ever on the look-out for this contradiction, because he knows that it is a foolproof way to prevent self-deception:

> It should be noted that when we feel an attachment opposed to actual poverty or a repugnance to it, when we are not indifferent to poverty and riches, it will be very helpful in order to overcome the inordinate attachment, even though corrupt nature rebel against it, to beg our Lord in the colloquies to choose us to serve him in actual poverty. We should insist that we desire it, beg for it, plead for it, provided, of course, that it be for the service and praise of Divine Goodness. (*Sp. Ex.*, 157)

Because Jesus is a sign of contradiction, in him are revealed the secrets of hearts (cf. Lk 2:35). *"Nothing is concealed that will not be revealed"* (Mt 10:26; Lk 12:2). In

---

with the worst kind of idols in 2 Kgs 23:24. —Ed.

a dramatic way, Jesus adhered to the will of his Father: this is how he fought, and this is how he conquered. In making his motto our own: *Father, not my will but yours be done*, in following as close behind his banner as possible, the revelation of many things that lie hidden in our heart will be brought to light. This is the only path that will not lead us astray when we seek to discern what we are feeling, where our heart is truly leading us…. It is the only sure path for discerning well.

Discernment of the lie by way of the Cross

The lie that grows

The lie, like all temptations of the Evil One, grows by itself. Satan invites us to "lay snares and bind with chains" (*Sp. Ex.*, 142), and he does so from a position of confusion and division (*confuse et divise*): "seated upon a great throne of fire and smoke" (*Sp. Ex.*, 140). From here issue the roots that nourish the growth of the lie in us: the self-sufficiency of our personal judgment and the fear born of human respect (cf. Jn 8:53-55; 9:41; 12:43).

The Demon, from the beginning, seeks to destroy man (Jn 8:44). Little by little, he prepares hearts, like that of Judas, instilling the desire for treason (Jn 13:2). The lie grows till it reaches the Cross, where it is definitively vanquished. In the measure that we adhere to the Cross of the Lord, in poverty, the desire for humiliation, and humility, we can defeat the lie of the Devil, and never let it grow again.

The truth of the Cross

The Cross reveals the good Spirit in its totality, since it is here that we behold the glory of the Word in the flesh. The Demon seeks to prevent this manifestation, this "hour" of the glorification of the Lord, because his original sin was to reject the Incarnation, the humiliation of the Word...and since he could not prevent it, he now tries to obstruct its glorious manifestation. The followers of the Demon are founded upon the lie (Jn 8:44; 1 Jn 2:22); they cannot open themselves to the knowledge of God (1 Jn 4:6). The love of God is not in them (1 Jn 2:15).

Once the Cross is manifested with the power of the Resurrection, then the lie loses strength, for its deceitful character is unmasked. It no longer possesses the power of fascination in itself, and must resort to "sordid commerce":

> *[The chief priests] assembled with the elders and took counsel; then they gave a large sum of money to the soldiers, telling them, "You are to say, 'His disciples came by night and stole him while we were asleep.' And if this gets to the ears of the governor, we will satisfy him and keep you out of trouble." The soldiers took the money and did as they were instructed. And this story has circulated among the Jews to the present day.* (Mt 28:12-15)

The lie and the lack of vigilance

When the servant lets his vigilance grow slack, his fidelity falls asleep. The one who in the beginning dozed off because he was lazy and cared little for the things of the Lord, ends by feigning sleep so as not to lose his pay. He can no longer distinguish between the restful, restorative sleep after an honest day's work and a comfortable, counterfeit, and corrupt slumber. Originating in the heart of an unfaithful servant in this way, the lie sets out to rearrange social relationships, as long as people are willing to "play possum." Thus, social sin gains a foothold and can hold sway from generation to generation, thanks to our capacity to work as sleepers for hire. Wherever we find deep-rooted social sins we discover dormant shepherds who have either sold their consciences or have simply lost the capacity to contemplate their Lord, because "*they could not keep their eyes open*" (Mt 26:43), and their hearts were "*sleeping from grief*" (Lk 22:45) out of fear of the Cross. Woe to the shepherds evade the Cross! In one way or another, they harbor the boastfulness of Peter in their hearts: "*Lord, I am prepared to go to prison and to die with you*" (Lk 22:33), or worse still: "*Even though all fall away, I will not*" (Mk 14:29 RSV).

Whoever is disposed to receive the Lord with all his heart will be able to know and follow the Lord.[28] On the other hand, hearts that are inattentive, distracted, and superficial, focused on anything but the essential, kill the desire for God and his mystery. Unlike these men who, like seed sown for the Kingdom but lost, fall on the footpath, on soil with little depth, full of rocks and thorns, and cannot bear fruit, there are also in the Church men

---

28   "Love justice, you who judge the earth;/ think of the LORD in goodness,/ and seek him in integrity of heart" (Wis 1:1).

and women of "great desires"[29] who, throughout their entire lives, look for — *what is more conducive* (*Sp. Ex.*, 23).

We are at the heart of the battle between the Two Standards. The Standard of Christ our Lord leads the way to poverty, a desire for insults and contempt, and humility. That of the Demon, the enemy of our human nature, seduces us with riches, vainglory, and pride. The Evil One will always try to make us long for the garlic and onions of Egypt, hoping we do not recall that this was the food of slavery (Nm 11:5).... Jesus will come to us with great gentleness speaking the Beatitudes. This battle takes place in me, it takes place among the nations, it takes place throughout history. Let us remember the words of Moses: *"See, I have today set before you life and good, death and evil"* (Dt 30:15).

We now conclude with a colloquy to our Lady:

> Asking her to obtain for me from her Son and Lord the grace to be received under his standard, first in the highest spiritual poverty, and should the Divine Majesty be pleased thereby, and deign to choose and accept me, even in actual poverty; secondly, in bearing insults and wrongs, thereby to imitate him better, provided only I can suffer these without sin on the part of another, and without offense of the Divine Majesty. Then I will say the *Hail Mary*. (*Sp. Ex.*, 147)

And I ask the same of the Son, and then the Father.

---

29   The author here makes reference to a passage from Saint Ignatius of Loyola's *Autobiography* (no. 14), in which the future founder of the Jesuits notes his "great desires to serve [Christ] in every way he knew." —Ed.

VIII
THE LORD WHO SENDS US ON A MISSION

The Lord, as "friend of our human nature," musters us and sends us into battle with the joy of true life. He sends us to *help* all men to live in the true happiness of the Kingdom, in the spirit of the Beatitudes:

> Consider how the Lord of all the world chooses so many persons, apostles, disciples, etc., and sends them throughout the whole world to spread his sacred doctrine among them, no matter what their state or condition. Consider the address our Lord makes to all his servants and friends whom he sends on this enterprise, recommending to them to seek to help all, first by attracting them to the highest spiritual poverty, and should it please the Divine Majesty, and should he deign to choose them for it, even to actual poverty. Secondly, they should lead them to a desire for insults and contempt, for from these springs humility. Hence, there will be three steps: the first, poverty as opposed to riches; the second, insults or contempt as opposed to the honor of this world; the third, humility as opposed to pride. From these three steps, let them lead to all other virtues. (*Sp. Ex.*, 146)

As Cardinal Martini says:

> This missionary mandate of the Lord is interesting. Curiously, he does not say: Call the greatest number of persons to the Church, have them baptized, believe, and come to Mass, but rather: Help all men, without exception, to free themselves from worrying about riches, from

the desire for recognition and fame that is fleeting, and from pride that kills love. The Lord, friend of human nature, charges his disciples to set all people free from the "nets and chains" of the devil. He charges them to help all to live in the freedom of the sons of God, rejecting all the ways the world enslaves, blinds, saddens, and causes anguish. It is the great commission from the Gospel of Mathew: *"Go, therefore, and make disciples of all nations, baptizing them in the name of the Father, and of the Son, and of the holy Spirit, teaching them to observe all that I have commanded you"* (Mt 28:19-20). He sends us to teach people how to live in the spirit of the Beatitudes that bring the freedom of heart that we all need: Christians and Protestants, Jews, Muslims, atheists, progressives and conservatives, and also those who are indifferent. This does not mean saying to the other: "Put aside your convictions and accept mine that are better," but rather to offer help, starting from the experience of Jesus without asking for anything in exchange, without setting down conditions. All men feel the need for the freedom Jesus teaches, even when one already has faith, we all need to be free ourselves from anguish and encounter peace and joy. It is this path of peace that we need to propose in a practical, ethical way, a way that leads man to decondition himself from all the daily oppressions of modern life.[30]

I would like us to pause here for a moment to meditate on two characteristic traits in the Lord's style of evangelization: joy and dialogue. He ardently desires that we make them our own.

---

30   Cardinal Maritini, *Mettere ordine nella propria vita*, 117ff. (Eng., *Letting God Free Us*).

The Lord who communicates to us the joy of evangelizing

Our joy in God is missionary joy—it is fervor:

"We have found the Messiah." (Jn 1:41)
"Then he brought him to Jesus." (Jn 1:42)
"We have found the one." (Jn 1:45)
"Go to my brothers and tell them." (Jn 20:17)

This joy of evangelizing is also consolation. It is a sign of the harmony and unity that is fulfilled in love. It is the sign of the unity of the Body of the Church, a sign of edification. We need to be faithful to the joy but not "enjoy" it for its own sake. This joy leads to wonder and impels us to share this wonder. Joy opens us to the freedom of the sons of God, separates us from the things and situations that imprison us, and helps us to grow in freedom through indifference.[31]

Joy is a sign of the Lord's presence, and should inform the habitual state of the consecrated man or woman. This means that we seek consolation,[32] not for its own sake, but because it is a sign of the presence of Christ. And Saint Ignatius teaches us that consolation comes in many forms:

---

31   Indifference, in the Ignatian sense of the word, is a preeminently positive spiritual attitude that founds us in true freedom and joy: "We must make ourselves indifferent to all created things" (Principle and Foundation, *Sp. Ex.*, 23). See chapter 2, p. 15, note 5.

32   In the *Spiritual Exercises*, it is by discerning the play of interior "movements"—consolation and desolation—that the retreatant comes to discover the specific path God wants him to follow. This process of discernment reflects what Saint Ignatius himself learned and practiced at the time of his conversion. —Ed.

I call it consolation when some interior movement is aroused in the soul, by which it is inflamed with love of its Creator and Lord, and as a consequence, can love no creature on the face of the earth for its own sake, but only in the Creator of them all. It is likewise consolation when one sheds tears that move to the love of God, whether it be because of sorrow for sins, or because of the sufferings of Christ our Lord, or for any other reason that is immediately directed to the praise and service of God. Finally, I call consolation every increase of faith, hope, and love, and all interior joy that invites and attracts to what is heavenly and to the salvation of one's soul by filling it with peace and quiet in its Creator and Lord. (*Sp. Ex.*, 316)

The sweet and comforting joy of evangelizing

Joy is fervor. Pope Paul VI ends *Evangelii nuntiandi* by speaking to us about this fervor:

Such obstacles are also present today, and we shall limit ourself to mentioning the lack of fervor. It is all the more serious because it comes from within. It is manifested in fatigue, disenchantment, compromise, lack of interest and above all lack of joy and hope. We exhort all those who have the task of evangelizing, by whatever title and at whatever level, always to nourish spiritual fervor.... Let us therefore preserve our fervor of spirit. Let us preserve the delightful and comforting joy of evangelizing, even when it is in tears that we must sow. May it mean for us...an interior enthusiasm that nobody and nothing can quench. May it be the great joy of our consecrated lives. And may the world of our time, which is searching, sometimes with anguish, sometimes with hope, be enabled to receive the Good News not from evangelizers who are dejected, discouraged, impatient or anxious, but from ministers of the Gospel whose lives glow with fervor, who have first received the joy of Christ. (*E.N.*, 80)[33]

This environment of joy is nourished by contemplating how Christ carried out his mission:

- how he walked
- how he preached
- how he cured
- how he gazed

The Lord shows us how to dialogue

In this joy of evangelizing, we will learn to dialogue like the Lord himself.

Let us first consider his dialogues with people. How Jesus talks:

- with those who want to impose their conditions
- with those who try to find fault with him
- with those who have their heart open to the hope of salvation

---

33 Pope John Paul II echoed this text in his encyclical letter *Redemptoris missio*, 91: "The missionary is a person of the Beatitudes. Before sending out the Twelve to evangelize, Jesus, in his 'missionary discourse' (cf. Mt 10), teaches them the paths of mission: poverty, meekness, acceptance of suffering and persecution, the desire for justice and peace, charity—in other words, the Beatitudes, lived out in the apostolic life (cf. Mt 5:1-12). By living the Beatitudes, the missionary experiences and shows concretely that the kingdom of God has already come, and that he has accepted it. The characteristic of every authentic missionary life is the inner joy that comes from faith. In a world tormented and oppressed by so many problems, a world tempted to pessimism, the one who proclaims the Good News must be a person who has found true hope in Christ."

Conditional dialogues

The three persons who present themselves to Jesus in Lk 9:57-62 lay down conditions for following him: their dialogues are *conditional*. They place limits on their commitment: riches, friends, father.

The Samaritan woman (Jn 4:1-41) tries to divert the dialogue because she does not want to touch the essential; she would rather talk about theology than her numerous "husbands."

As for Nicodemus (Jn 3:1-21), security is the condition he imposes for an encounter with Jesus: he comes under the cover of night to ask him questions. And Jesus, because he senses that the Pharisee is not well disposed, lets him remain wrapped up in his trivial objections. For Nicodemus, such objections serve as an egoistic refuge for not being honest.

Deceptive dialogues

There exists another group of dialogues with Jesus: *deceptive* dialogues. These involve attempts to "entrap" the Lord, in order to find cracks in his coherence. This would then permit a piety conceived along the lines of a trade-off: faith for security, hope for possessions, love for egoism. For example, in the scene with the adulterous woman (Jn 8:1-11), if Jesus says yes, then his mercy is disqualified; if he says no, then he contradicts the law.

In these deceptive dialogues Jesus usually does two things: he speaks a word of doctrine to the one trying to entrap him, and a different word to the victim (in this case, the adulterous woman) or, in certain instances, he addresses the deceptive situation in itself. Here, he both confounds and condemns his entrappers, telling them to apply the law to themselves. To the woman he returns her life, lovingly but firmly telling her to assume responsibility for it.

In the same sense we can meditate upon the episode with the baited question about paying tribute to Caesar. It is a question that leads one to believe there is no alternative between the Saduccean temptation of collaboration with the State (Mt 22:15-22) and that of rebellion against authority (Lk 20:1-8). The Lord responds by exhorting his detractors to assume responsibility for the "authorities" whom God has sent them, but whom they have not accepted.

There is another trap, set by the Saduccees again, to which the Lord responds by directing his gaze to eschatological horizons (Lk 20:27-40): the woman who had seven husbands and the question of the resurrection. When the hardness of the deceitful heart is irreversible, then it involves a mortal sin, a sin against the Holy Spirit: their spirits lie in darkness. It is such a sordid snare that the Lord refuses to dignify their dialectic with a response; he simply turns to the purity of his glory, and from there offers his reply.

The root of all deceit is always vainglory, possessions, sensuality, pride. And the Lord himself taught us to respond to these deceptive temptations with the joyful story of the faithful people of God (Mt 4:1-11).

Honest dialogues

Finally there is a third group of dialogues with Jesus that we can call *honest* dialogues. These take place with those who approach Jesus without duplicity; their hearts are upright and open to the manifestation of God. Nothing is hidden under the table. When someone comes to Jesus in this way, his heart is filled with joy (Lk 10:21). Let us meditate often on the dialogue between Christ and the man born blind (Jn 9:1-41).

True joy is forged in work, in the Cross. The joy that has not been tested is nothing more than simple enthusiasm, often indiscreet, and whose fruitfulness is far from certain. Jesus prepares us for this test, and he warns us so that we may be ready to stand fast and persevere: *"So you also are now in anguish. But I will see you again, and your hearts will rejoice, and no one will take your joy away from you"* (Jn 16:22). Saint Ignatius also exhorts us to defeat temptation and desolation with constant work and hope in future consolation:

> When one is in desolation, he should strive to persevere in patience. This reacts against the vexations that have overtaken him. Let him consider, too, that consolation will soon return, and in the meantime, he must diligently use the means against desolation which have been given in the sixth rule.[34] (*Sp. Ex.*, 321)

---

34 This is the eighth rule for the discernment of spirits in the first week of the *Spiritual Exercises*. —Ed.

IX
THE LORD WHO REFORMS US

The Lord who prunes and purifies: The Three Classes of Men[35]

When, in the *Spiritual Exercises* (149-157), Saint Ignatius places before us these three groups of persons, or "classes of men" as he calls them, he is offering more than mere examples of three spiritual attitudes. As a brilliant strategist of the Kingdom, Ignatius knows very well that "only the kingdom is absolute and it makes everything else relative." In fact, "the kingdom of God...is so important that, by comparison, everything else becomes 'the rest,' which is 'given in addition' [cf. Mt 6:33]" (*E.N.*, 8). He knows that the Lord demands of us "a total interior renewal which the Gospel calls *metanoia*; it is a radical conversion, a profound change of mind and heart [cf. Mt 4:17]" (*E.N.*,10).

Saint Ignatius is also keenly aware that Jesus' "words reveal the secret of God, his plan and his promise, and thereby change the heart of man and his destiny" (*E.N.*, 11). Thus, by placing us before the radicality of the message of Jesus, Ignatius gives us a glimpse of

---

35 Before making his or her election—or choice—the retreatant is called to meditate upon the spiritual attitude of the three groups of men: each has acquired ten thousand ducats, an enormous sum, but not entirely as they should have, for the love of God. The aim of this meditation is to put into practice what the Principle and Foundation calls indifference (*Sp. Ex.*, 23), that is, to help the retreatant overcome any attachment that stands in the way of following the will of God.—Ed.

the challenging mission that the Lord has entrusted to his Church: "the Church evangelizes when she seeks to convert…both the personal and collective consciences of people, the activities in which they engage, and the lives and concrete milieu which are theirs" (*E.N.*, 18).

Two things are clear:

– First, the message of Jesus is absolute, and we must therefore examine our consciences anew to verify personally whether "everything else is truly everything else."

– Second, that its very radicality aims at "transforming humanity from within and making it new…. But there is no new humanity if there are not first of all new men renewed by Baptism and by lives lived according to the Gospel" (*E.N.*, 18).

For this reason Saint Ignatius, just prior to the election, places us before whatever might obscure the radicality of the Gospel: he places us before the famous ten thousand ducats—the "sum acquired" (*Sp. Ex.*, 150). And all of us have acquired such "sums." This is the moment to ask ourselves: What is my acquired sum? Now is the time to call it by name so that I am not dominated by it, but dominated rather by the Lord (*Dominus*). More concretely still, let us ask ourselves what are the "acquired sums" that act as obstacles to our mission as pastors, that impede our institutionalization in service of the Church, as we discussed earlier.[36]

---

36 See the section in chapter 5 entitled "The apostolic constancy that creates institutions," p. 55-57. —Ed.

We will indicate some possibilities that might serve as a helpful guide.

My hegemony

My hegemony leads me to confuse the part with the whole: to think that what is mine, what I am doing, is the only valid and viable way the Church should be working in the here and now.

We realize, however, that it is impossible to be a living body, to be a truly living and breathing institution, unless we accept and love the body of the whole Church. Thus, as pastors, we must continually cultivate this living awareness that our activity, whatever it may be, is only a part and not the whole of the Church's apostolic work.

To pretend that we are all the same, that there are "radical options" for everyone in this or that given field, is precisely to distance ourselves from the true radicality of the Gospel. It is to imagine that what saves us is the activity I am doing, the approach I am taking, with the priorities I have set down.

Very often we would like it if more young people would come join us in the work we are doing, and that they would carry it forward into the future. But we see that they are called to do other things, seemingly unremarkable work, like taking care of the elderly, or teaching young children.... When our heart is closed in its own project, thinking it is self-sufficient, we are incapable of seeing how the work of fortifying young hearts, or showing tenderness to the elderly, is a treasure for the institutional Body. At other times we are sorely disappointed when we can't count on our brothers as collaborators, when their tasks almost seem to us like exercises in futility. Yet many times futility is another name for victory—many times it means rescuing a brother.

All of this can lead to a type of apostolic pride, which is not the same thing as a healthy recognition that God works through us, using us as instruments of "consolation" for many of our brothers. It is a type of pride that can make us want to be "in the news," part of the "buzz," always "in the know" and "on top of things." And this can lead us to be closed off, not open and reasonable about all that is happening in the diocese or in the Church: the problems of others, the health of the elderly and infirm, the care and formation of the young…

If my "acquired sum" is this desire for my own hegemony, then we should have no illusions that we will somehow find solutions by talking about pluralism. Here the only admissable pluralism is that of the apostolic mission we have received: this is what founds unity, and makes us brothers. There is no room for pluralism apart from the Head and the Body: any other pluralism is just disguised hegemony.

My conscience

My conscience becomes an "acquired sum" when I defend it as such, abstracted from the sense of belonging to the body of the Church, divorced from the conscience of the faithful. This occurs when we confuse dogmatism with doctrine, resignation with pastoral leadership. Then we fall into the familiar attitudes that harm the people of God. For example, when I think that "I am the one who knows what is right, and the faithful lack one because they are ignorant, stupid, etc." Then, instead of guiding the flock I end up giving them orders. Or, conversely: "I have no idea what I should do in this situation, but the people do," and thus I shirk my pastoral responsibilities. Beneath these two attitudes lie hidden assumptions:

- "I am not the people"
- "The people can't be led"
- "The people don't need a pastor"
- "The pastor should only obey the people"
- "The people don't know anything," etc.

When my conscience is clearly out of touch with the conscience of the portion of God's faithful people entrusted to my care, it is time to ask myself about my "acquired sum." What am I defending through this kind of isolation? A pastoral dictatorship? A precious role that makes me the flock's "hairdresser" rather then their pastor? The pastoral reality is this: people want religion to bring them closer to God; they want a priest to be a shepherd, not a tyrant or a dandy who loses himself in the frills of fashion.

At times we express this in terms of "my experience." Personal experience certainly carries value, but we can use it badly. For example, my experience of many years of pastoral work, almost self-taught in this area, can lead me to anchor myself in my own wisdom, in "my experience" and not the inspiration of the Holy Spirit. I come to know it all, handling things with ease, but above the people, with no need to consult with anyone about my problems, or about my pastoral plans…or about my ineffectiveness, since I have not formed Christians who can act on their own without me.

Behind these "acquired sums" we can detect an incredible spirit of self-sufficiency. Without going to the extreme of those who "with lamentable superficiality accuse the Church of having made a detour from her essential evangelizing mission,"[37] we frequently fall into the trap of self-sufficiency, which undermines the growth and unity of the body of the Church. And the worst is "to believe that one has definitively reached Christ." This amounts to "assurance in oneself and contempt for others," "when each one believes that he has the infallible key for solving all the problems; when, for example, in the Church some believe that they are the only poor ones and have understood the Gospel, that they have discovered the secret to become more transparent and closer to Jesus Christ, that they are the only ones really committed to the liberation of man, while others think that they are the only ones faithful to the richness of the Tradition or set themselves up as infallible teachers of their brothers."

This spirit of self-sufficiency is born of the Evil One, the father of lies who, by this path, transmits tensions, divisions, and dismemberment to the Church. Thus, we can be sure that "tensions often come from a supposedly exclusive right to truth and holiness. Peace can only enter

---

37 Cardinal Eduardo Pironio, *Meditación para tiempos difíciles* [*Meditation on Difficult Times*], op. cit., 2-9.

into hearts that are open and disponible; and disponibility presupposes poverty."

Being poor means not having "acquired sums."

My power

Here we touch upon another "acquired sum": my power—the kind I would like in my pastoral work, but which Christ has not given me. For example, encroaching upon and "borrowing" the power of others, or, conversely, believing that pastoral work should have absolutely nothing to do with power. Whichever form it takes, such an attitude distances us from the true power Christ has conferred upon us: to baptize, to teach doctrine and help put it into practice, to bless, heal, pardon, etc. (cf. Mt 28:19-20; Jn 20:22-23; Mk 16:15-18).

My immobility

My immobility, whether it be in terms of location or attitude, can act as another "acquired sum" that stands in the way of total service to the Lord. This way of saying, "I obey, but within this perimeter, this diocese, this place," strikes at the very root of the institution, because it privileges fixed comfort, which is always less convenient but fruitful, to being "sent on a mission."

We could continue adding to this list of "acquired sums" and create an entire catalog. Each one of you has to look into your heart (for precisely there is the path) and see where your treasure lies, your "acquired sum." In doing so, let us remember the other "acquisition," which

Christ has gained for us, *"a people he claims for his own to proclaim the glorious works of the One who called you from darkness into his marvelous light"* (1 Pt 2:9). Let us call to mind the concrete faces of the people in our dioceses who have been entrusted to us as pastors, and let us compare the two acquisitions: what my stingy heart holds dear and what Christ has won for us. And then let us decide.

Let us also remember that every "acquired sum" militates against the unity of the Church, dividing in order to sow confusion. What separates us from the harmony of the Body of the Bride of Christ is always something paltry that we want to keep for ourselves. By contrast, the constant effort to foster concord and unity gives flight to the demons of division and fortifies our membership in the Church. Saint Ignatius of Antioch offers a similar reminder to the Ephesians (ch. 13): "Be eager for more frequent celebrations of the Eucharist and the divine praises. For when you meet frequently the forces of Satan are annulled and his destructive power is cancelled in the concord of your faith. There is nothing better than peace, in which all hostility is abolished, whether it comes from the powers of heaven or the powers of earth."

And may the Lord grant us the grace "neither to want that, nor anything else, unless the service of God our Lord alone move us to do so," as Saint Ignatius of Loyola says, speaking of the third class of men who succeeded in detaching themselves from all things so as to desire to serve God our Lord above all else (*Sp. Ex.*, 155).

X

THE LORD WHO ANOINTS US: "THE THREE KINDS OF HUMILITY"[38]

> Children, it is the final hour; just as you heard that the Antichrist was coming, so now many such antichrists have appeared. This makes us certain that it is the final hour.... But you have the anointing that comes from the Holy One, so that all knowledge is yours.... As for you, the anointing you received from him remains in your hearts. This means you have no need for anyone to teach you. Rather, as his anointing teaches you about all things and is true—free from any lie—remain in him as that anointing has taught you. (1 Jn 2:18, 20, 27)

Every age is beset by difficulties, and the life of the believer is no different. Our best recourse in the face of these inevitable difficulties is the same one the Lord gave us in the Gospel: *"I bid you resolve not to worry about your defence beforehand, for I will give you words and a wisdom which none of your adversaries can withstand or contradict"* (Lk 21:14-15). Our recourse will be the anointing.

Saint John reminds us that "the final hour" is an eschatological moment. It is the hour of the Antichrist, of the false prophets (Mt 24:11), but it is also the hour of

---

38   This meditation is proposed to the retreatant just before making the choice of a way of life. The retreatant knows that this will entail renunciation (we recall the three classes of men), but he or she still needs to discover that there can be no genuine renunciation without love, that is to say, without poverty and without humility (*Sp. Ex.*, 165-168). Yet humility itself also admits of degrees. —Ed.

the coming of Christ. In a certain sense, it is every hour of Christ's coming in our lives and the reactions it elicits. In order to be faithful to all these eschatological moments, we are asked not to forget the anointing we have received.

Those who have grown tired of the humble Christ or ways of rejecting the vocation to the Cross

The antichrists are in our very midst: some of us have become weary of the humility of Christ. Belonging to Christ is not simply a matter of being physically part of a community. It goes much further than that. It means belonging to the Spirit, letting oneself be anointed by the same Spirit who anointed Jesus.

Our belonging is determined by our anointing in Christ, by the Lord himself who is *"well aware of what is in man's heart"* (cf. Jn 2:24-25). When Christ is received into a man's heart, that person becomes a source of division (Mt 10:21). It is a sign of the end times (Lk 21:28). The believer becomes like Christ himself, one *"destined to be the downfall and the rise of many in Israel, a sign of contradiction"* (cf. Lk 2:34). One who has not received the anointing, who does not accept it or who compensates for it with mere human science, can in fact deny the vocation to the Cross.

Choosing one's own signs of contradiction

One of the principal ways of denying the Cross is the attitude of choosing for oneself the signs of contradiction. The Cross, then, is no longer an offering of one's own life, following the Lord in love down the path he first chose to take, but rather superficial posturing, "putting on a show," a sham. We have seen many priests and religious who, in their community life, "play the primitive Church game," or others who "play the Cross" in their apostolic life. In such cases, the persecution that may result is not the fruit of zeal for the glory of the Father, for fulfilling the will of God. It is rather an exquisitely artificial and elitist selection of the means that, in a vain and egoistic spirit, seem most expedient at that moment.

Rejecting the combative character of the vocation: irenicism

The second way of denying our vocation to the Cross is rooted in rejection of the combative character of our vocation. This is the temptation of "Peace at any cost," the temptation of irenicism. This temptation springs from fear of contradiction, and one resorts to any and every type of accomodation or compromise in order to achieve peace. Peace thus becomes the absence of contradiction. The result: men and women do not benefit from real peace at all, but rather live in cowardice, or, if you like, the peace of the grave.

Those who go beyond the doctrine of the community

The two aforementioned temptations are rooted in the desire—which one refuses to relinquish—to cast themselves as the protagonists of the Cross, in the first case, and of peace, in the second. One forgets that both the Cross and peace already have a Protagonist who has fulfilled and given meaning to the path of salvation, both in the Passion as well as in the consolation of the Resurrection. These two groups of people, enemies of the Cross of Christ, overstep or "go beyond" the doctrine of the community (cf. 2 Jn 9). They invent an alternative tailored to the size of their egoism, they are delirious and hallucinate, *"defile the flesh, reject authority, and revile the glorious ones"* (Jude 8 RSV).

Assured in Christ

In the midst of divisions and attitudes contrary to the Cross of the Lord, our security is rooted in the anointing. It is the Word received, and internalized. Through the anointing we receive all knowledge, and it teaches us about everything (1 Jn 2:27). The anointing places us in the truth. Remaining in Jesus we will know the truth (Jn 8:32). The lie is Satan. It is not a matter of multiplying instructions, but of recognizing how in this anointing, in this *"sensus fidelium,"* we truly belong to the Body of Christ.

The anointing is the reality of the end times, when it will be given to everyone (cf. Jer 31:34). In times of true contradiction, we need to remember the promise of the Lord: *"I will inspire you with wisdom"* (cf. Lk 21:15; 12:12). Because the anointing is wisdom, we must ask for it (Wis 9:5-12). Through the anointing we are *assured* in Christ (2 Cor 1:21). The anointing gives us a solidity and certainty that cannot be confounded (Heb 6:19; Lk 1:4; Phil 3:1).

The anointing brings to perfection

The Lord calls us to anoint what needs to be perfected and cured: the dead are anointed (Mk 16:1); the sick are anointed (Mk 6:13; Jas 5:14); wounds are anointed (Lk 10:34); penitents are anointed (Mt 6:17). The anointing also carries the sense of reparation: Lk 7:38, 46; 10:34; Jn 11:2; 12:3. All these senses hold validity for us: we are resurrected, cured, reformed, and repaired by the anointing of the Holy One. The yoke of slavery is destroyed by means of the anointing (cf. Is 10:27).

The first to be anointed is the Lord (Lk 2:26; 4:18; Acts 4:26; 10:38). He was anointed with the *"oil of gladness"* (Heb 1:9). Gladness evokes glory.[39] To be anointed means to participate in the glory of Christ, which is his Cross. *"The hour has come for the Son of Man to be glorified... Father, glorify your name!"* (Jn 12:23, 28). Conversely, those who seek peace or contradiction apart from the anointing, do not seek the glory of God on the Cross of Christ: *"How can you believe, who receive glory from one another and do not seek the glory that comes from the only God?"* (Jn 5: 44 RSV)

To desire or be disposed to suffer patiently

When Saint Ignatius asks us to meditate upon the "three grades of humility," his aim is to lead us to this anointing in its utmost radicality: the culmination of wisdom—the Cross of Christ (*Sp. Ex.*, 165-168).

Ignatius makes the following crucial point in this regard:

> In the second week, which is concerned with elections, the aim of the retreatants should not be to deliberate over the state of life that has been chosen. Rather than

---

39   Saint Cyril of Jerusalem, *Catechetical Lecture* 13.

reflections of this kind, propose that they choose one of two things: the first, all things being equal in the divine service and without committing an offense or harming one's neighbor, is to desire insults, contempt, and to be humiliated with Christ in everything so as to be clad in his uniform, and imitating him in this part of his Cross; or, the second, to be disposed to suffer patiently, for the love of Christ our Lord, anything akin to what he suffered.[40]

The field of combat, so to speak, where the election of a state of life takes place, is in reality a dramatic battle-ground of desire: it is where we desire insults and contempt, or are disposed to accept them, all for the love of Christ. This is the Glory, this is the Wisdom, and this is the anointing that teaches us the way to go without fail.

Let us listen to the apt invitation of Saint Augustine:

> We return, then, to that anointing of Christ, to that unction which inwardly teaches us what we of ourselves are unable to express, and—because it is impossible to see—let our part and task be in desire. The whole life of the Christian is a holy desire.[41]

In the measure that we are anointed by the wisdom of the Cross, our heart is made wider by the desire for great things: like Christ on the Cross, our heart too is opened. The fruitful magnanimity that "always goes beyond," that

---

40 Ignatius offers this advice in the autograph *Directory of the Spiritual Exercises*, a set of further instructions for retreat masters (see chapter 3, n. 23, Concerning Elections); emphasis added by Jorge Mario Bergoglio. —Ed.
41 Saint Augustine, Homily 4 on the First Letter of John.

seeks "only what is more conducive" (*Sp. Ex.*, 23), is a daughter of the Cross.

Contemplating the Lord stretched upon the Cross, his heart wide open, and his Blessed Mother standing by his side, we beg for the grace to be anointed to follow him, to be crucified with him. We beg that our heart may be saved from the stinginess that makes us puny and close-fisted — that it may learn, in the anointing of the Cross, the measure of great desires, which are instruments of fecundity in service of our Holy Mother the Church.

XI
THE LORD,
OUR DEATH AND RESURRECTION

The Cross of the Lord

Once the choice (or reform) of our state of life is made, we approach the Cross of our Lord and place ourselves at his feet, pressed fast to the wood. We beg him to grant us the strength to soldier on, following in his footsteps to the rhythm of an ancient adage that recapitulates the dynamic of the *Spiritual Exercises*:

Deformata reformare–to reform what was deformed by sin

Reformata conformare–to configure what was reformed to the Lord's life

Conformata confirmare–to fortify what was configured with the Passion and Cross of the Lord

Confirmata transformare–to transform what was confirmed in the light of the Resurrection

Christ was anointed on the Cross. We dedicate this meditation to the contemplation of the wood of the Cross. Just as it is—rough-hewn and raw, stripped of the corpus of Christ. This hard wood that impresses itself upon the flesh, and down to the very marrow of all who would advance under the Standard of the King.

Over the centuries, campaigns of deceit and persecution have been waged against the Cross, pounding upon it like waves, dashing themselves into froth and foam.

Against it have broken all forms of Messianic fraud, all non-Christian hopes, all egoism disguised as generosity and good will. The Cross of Christ is a beacon, beckoning us to embrace the *Way, the Truth, and the Life* made flesh. For non-believers, the Cross is but a scandal and a disgrace—a mere gallows where crimes meet with ghastly retribution. For us, it is something altogether Other: the shining Standard of glory. Yes, it calls for surrender and self-emptying, an intimate *kenosis* (Phil 2:6-11). But this is precisely why the Cross is our only hope (*Spes unica*).

And so it goes with the things of the Lord, with the Cross: we grasp its true gravity and grandeur according to the "spirit" with which we cast our gaze upon it. In matters of faith, we always have ready at hand some human "reason" or "interpretation" for not accepting the message of the Lord. At times we think we know it all, which quickly leads to knowing nothing at all. Often we are like the disciples of Emmaus: they think they know the Lord so well, yet when they encounter him along the way, they do not even recognize his face.

Let us spend some time together in contemplation, resting our gaze upon the bare wood of the Cross. Letting go of our preconceptions and prior knowledge, let us allow this naked tree to speak to us and challenge us: "Here is the wisdom you seek, the key for interpreting life, hope raised high for all to see."

The people of God is an "army corps," the Christian life is combat. But *"our battle is not against human forces but against the principalities and powers, the rulers of this world of darkness, the evil spirits in regions above*" (Eph 6:12). In order to win this battle, human weapons are useless. We need to put on the "armor of God" in order to "resist and stand our ground." And God's most powerful weapon is the Cross. It is with these mighty arms that the Evil One suffered defeat once and for all. When we take up the cross as our Standard of salvation, we sense deep down that "*the battle is not ours but God's*" (cf. 2 Chr 20:15), and that he is the one who is fighting for us. This grace is given to us when in humility—the humility of recognizing that we need to be saved—we cling fast to the Cross. When we learn that our glory lies in embracing our weakness, then the power of Christ can take root in us:

> *Therefore, I am content with weakness, with mistreatment, with distress, with persecutions and difficulties for the sake of Christ; for when I am powerless, it is then that I am strong.* (2 Cor 12:10)

The mystery of the Cross springs from this paradox: only the "weak" and the "little ones" are in a position to comprehend it, only those who forsake every other hermeneutic of life and who know that they have to "*let the dead bury their dead*" (Mt 8:22). What a challenge this wisdom is–that only in weakness and humility can we understand the Cross! In this search for poverty rather than riches, humiliation rather than vanity, and humility rather than pride, we recognize the Pauline invitation to take up the Cross, which is a "*scandal for the Jews and folly for the pagans*" (cf. 1 Cor 1:23). Following the Apostle, Saint Ignatius does not hesitate to propose that the retreatant become "a fool for Christ" (*Sp. Ex.*, 167).

Let us pause a moment and ponder the Pauline invitation to "foolishness," "weakness," and "littleness," as elaborated by Ignatius in the Constitutions of the Society of Jesus:

> It is likewise very important to bring to the attention of those who are being examined, emphasizing it and giving it great weight in the sight of our Creator and Lord, to how great a degree it helps and profits in the spiritual life to abhor in its totality and not in part whatever the world loves and embraces, and to accept and desire with all possible energy whatever Christ our Lord has loved and embraced. Just as the men of the world who follow the world love and seek with great diligence honors, fame, and esteem for a great name on earth, as the world teaches them, so those who proceed spiritually and truly follow Christ our Lord love and desire intensely everything opposite. That is to say, they desire to clothe themselves with the same garb and uniform of their Lord because of the love and reverence owed to him, to such an extent that where there would be no offense to his Divine Majesty and no imputation of sin to the neighbor, they desire to suffer injuries, false accusations, and affronts, and to be held and esteemed as fools (but without giving any occasion for this), because of their desire to resemble and imitate in some manner our Creator and Lord Jesus Christ, by putting on his garb and uniform, since it was for our spiritual profit that he clothed himself as he did. For he gave us an example that in all things possible to us we might seek, with the aid of his grace, to imitate and follow him, since he is the way which leads all men and women to life." (General Examen, *Const.* 101)

This littleness of the Kingdom entails self-emptying, which will grow ever more demanding over the course of our life. It is not by chance that, in the midst of the peace and joy of the Resurrection, Jesus reminds Peter that he must follow him in complete surrender:

> *As a young man you fastened your belt and went about as you pleased; but when you are older you will stretch out your hands, and another will tie you fast and carry you off against your will.* (Jn 21:18)

Our temptation is the same as Peter's: to look around for another way, losing oneself in the details. *"But Lord, what about him?"* (pointing to the Apostle John, Jn 21:21). May God, in his great bounty, grant us the grace to repeat in our ear the words Peter received in reply, and to remind us of our vocation to self-surrender: *"What concern is it of yours? You follow me"* (Jn 21:22). Let us look to the Cross alone, a gibbet to some, gibberish to others, but for us the very power of God.

And let us take the time now to savor the following lines that Saint Theodore the Studite addressed to his monks:

> O infinitely precious gift of the Cross! How beautiful to behold! The beauty it unfurls is not fraught with good and evil as the Eden-tree of old. It is entirely admirable and delectable, to sight and taste alike. Indeed, this tree engenders life and not death; light and not darkness. It bids us enter the Garden gates afresh, to be banished from its delights no more. Such is the tree Christ scaled on high, a King astride his battle chariot;

such is the wood that felled the Fiend, delivering mankind from the tyrant's grip, which once did wield the blade of doom. From the heights of his Triumph-tree did our valiant warrior Lord—battle scars agleam upon hands, feet, and divinely streaming side—bend down to bind the wounds of sin. This I mean did mend our human nature mortally mauled by the infernal Beast. After suffering death by tainted tree, by blood-stained rood we dream of life anew; after tasting from deceptive branch, limbs of grace redress our shame, and give the deceitful serpent chase. What strange and marvelous exchange! Life in place of death, immortality in place of decay, glory in place of disgrace! Not without cause did the Apostle exclaim: May I glory in aught but the Cross of Christ alone, through which the world has been crucified to me, and I to the world! For the wisdom born of the Cross has laid bare the vain pretense the world calls wisdom. The knowledge of all good that blossoms forth from the Cross has severed the roots of every flower of evil.

From the beginning of the world, all those things that were but shadowy figures or anticipations of this wood, cried out as clues or signs of something infinitely more admirable than themselves. Look then, you who desire to know. Was it by chance that Noah escaped the deluge through God's decision—he, his wife, his sons and their wives, with animals of every stripe—riding out the waves on a fragile raft of gopher wood? And what did the staff of Moses signify? Is it not a figure of the Cross? When it changed water into blood, when it devoured the false serpents of the magicians, when he smote the waters and clove the sea in twain, surging back to swallow the enemy whole, and rescue the chosen people.

The staff of Aaron too is a figure of the Cross, armed with like vigor as it burst into bloom in a single day, thus confirming who was the legitimate priest. Abraham likwise announced the Cross, when he laid his bound son upon an altar of wood. By the Cross death was destroyed, and Adam restored to life. All the Apostles gloried in the Cross, all the Martyrs were crowned by the Cross, and all the Saints were sanctified by the Cross. By the Cross we put on Christ, and put away the old man. Through the Cross, we, Christ's sheep, have been gathered into the same enclosure, and are destined for the heavenly sheephold.[42]

From the Cross, let us now go to the house of our Lady, where she suffers in solitude, and let us recite with her the hymn that an Argentinian pastor composed for Lent:

Holy Cross of Christ, Tree of Life:
The King has driven out vanquished death.

Holy Cross of Christ, Covenant and Pardon:
Strength of the poor, riches of God.

Holy Cross of Christ, standing steadfast by your Lord:
While all things pass away, be our support.

Holy Cross of Christ, Sacrificial Lamb:
Wash us from the wound in your open side.

Holy Cross of Christ, mystery of love:
Guide our steps to the Kingdom of God.

Holy Cross of Christ, O open arms:
Reunite your people dispersed throughout the world.

---

42 Saint Theodore the Studite, *Oratio* II (*In Adorationem Crucis*), *Patrologia Græca*, ed. J.-P. Migne (Paris, 1860), vol. 99, 691-699.

Holy Cross of Christ, beacon to every Christian:
We adore you, O Christ,
And we give you glory![43]

The peace of the resurrected Lord

This is how we shall know that we belong to the truth and reassure our hearts before him in whatever our hearts condemn, for God is greater than our hearts and knows everything. (1 Jn 3:19-20)

In the fourth week of the *Spiritual Exercises*, Saint Ignatius has us contemplate the resurrected Jesus in his role as *consoler* to his friends. The Lord consoles by making himself present in the midst of the community and showing his resurrected wounds, wounds flowing forth with peace, peace that conquers all our fears.

The greeting of the resurrected Christ, *"Peace be with you"* (Jn 20:19, 26) is the watchword of definitive triumph. To participate in this peace, to receive it, means to participate already in the peace of the Resurrection. Peace should be the habitual state of a religious, a priest, a bishop because—as a mediator — he has his heart anchored in the ultimate good, in the "goods on high." "That our hearts may be firmly fixed where true joys are to be found," we pray in the liturgy.

We must not confuse true peace with the illusion of peace. This latter is the peace of ignorance, the peace of feigned innocence that dances around difficulties, the

---

43   Fernando Boasso, s.J., Primer Viernes de Cuaresma [First Friday of Lent], 1977.

peace of the rich man Dives who ignores Lazarus. True peace grows out of the tension between two contrary elements: the acceptance of a present in which we recognize our weakness as sinners, and, at the same time, passing beyond the same present as if we were already freed from the burden of sin. Saint Ignatius invites us on several occasions to enter into this explicit tension in his "theology of the as if." "As if I were there," he counsels, encouraging us to contemplate this or that scene from the Gospel; imagining ourselves, for example, at the Nativity, "as though present" beside Christ in the manger (*Sp. Ex.*, 110). And in order to make a good election or choice, we are to do so "as if" we were making it at the moment of our death or on the day of Judgment (*Sp. Ex.*, 186-187). The locus of this peace is the heart: it is here that the presence of Jesus gives us assurance.

This peace is the foundation and wellspring of apostolic courage (*parrhesia*) and apostolic patience (*hypomone*). To live this peace does not mean maintaining tranquility! We are not talking about an easy peace, but rather a demanding one. Peace does not eliminate fragility or deficiencies. This peace enables us to choose a state of life and to do God's will. It is not the peace the world gives (Jn 14:27) but the peace of the Lord (Jn 16:33).

Our God is the God of peace (Rom 15:33). He desired to give us this peace, by pacifying us in his Son (Rom 5:1), so that we too would transmit it in turn, as the bond of communion that preserves unity (Eph 4:3). The advent of this peace was made known to all on Christmas Eve

(Lk 2:14), and the echo of this announcement resounds all the way to Palm Sunday (Lk 19:38). We have been asked to seek it, and to direct our feet *"into the way of peace"* (Lk 1:79), for all of us have been called to live in peace (1 Cor 7:15). May this peace guard our hearts and minds (Phil 4:7) and inspire us to seek peace with all men and women (Heb 12:14). To reject this peace separates us from the fear of God (Rom 3:17-18) and grieves the heart of Christ (Lk 19:42).

Peace is a Beatitude (Mt 5:9), and we seek it because, in it and with it, we must wage war for the Kingdom. The Lord tells us: He has come to bring war (Mt 10:34). We are called to participate in this war he wages, for he granted a certain degree of power to the Demon to take away peace from the earth (Rv 6:4). In the end, however, the God of peace will crush Satan (Rm 16:20).

In this war against evil, peace fortifies our courage, and does not let us be intimidated by our adversaries (Phil 1:28). Above all, peace determines our "style of combat," a style that is born in peace, battles in peace, and engenders peace:

> But if you have bitter jealousy and selfish ambition in your hearts, do not boast and be false to the truth. Wisdom of this kind does not come down from above but is earthly, unspiritual, demonic. For where jealousy and selfish ambition exist, there is disorder and every foul practice. But the wisdom from above is first of all pure, then peaceable, gentle, compliant, full of mercy and good fruits, without inconstancy or insincerity.

> *And the fruit of righteousness is sown in peace for those who cultivate peace.* (Jas 3:14-18)

In our meditations on the mysteries of the Resurrection, let us take some time to gaze upon Christ as the protagonist of peace. This is what Saint Ignatius means when he asks us to "consider the office of consoler that Christ our Lord exercises, and compare it with the way friends are wont to console each other" (*Sp. Ex.*, 224). Peace is rooted in consolation: only one who has allowed himself to be consoled by the Lord knows how to console others.

Finally, let us feel the Lord's profound gaze of goodness come to rest upon us. He knows everything, and with tenderness he tells us: "*Your faith has saved you. Go in peace*" (Mk 5:34; Lk 7:50; 8:48).

XII
THE LORD WHO TRANSFORMS US WITH HIS LOVE

Memory

Contemplation to attain love

When Saint Ignatius asks us to renew our memory of "the blessings of creation and redemption, and the special favors I have received" (*Sp. Ex.*, 234), he wants us to go much further than merely giving thanks for all that we have received. He wants to teach us to have *more love*. He wants to confirm and strengthen us on the path we have chosen, and what enables this is memory. Memory is like the grace of the presence of the Lord in our lives. The memory of the past that we carry within us, not as a weight, but as a reality interpreted in the light of our current circumstances and awareness. Let us ask for the grace to recover the memory:

- of our personal journey of faith
- of the ways the Lord has come looking for us
- of our religious family
- of the people entrusted to our care as bishops

Exercising our memory makes us more awake, so to speak, and enables us to receive the word of God with greater power: *"Recall the days gone by when, after you had been enlightened, you endured a great contest of suffering.... Do not, then, surrender your confidence"* (Heb 10:32, 35).

"Remember your leaders who spoke the word of God to you; consider how their lives ended, and imitate their faith" (Heb 13:7). This memory safeguards us from getting *"carried away by all kinds of strange teaching"* (Heb 13:9), and thus *"fortifies our faith"* (cf. Heb 13:9).

Peoples also have a memory, just like persons. Mankind too shares a common memory. On the faces of the Mataco Indians, for instance, we witness the living memory of a suffering and persecuted race.[44] In the voice of the people of La Rioja we hear Saint Nicholas.[45] Archbishop Tavella recounted that in a village in his diocese he found an Indian who was praying with great intensity. After a long while, the bishop asked him what he was praying. "The Catechism," replied the Indian. It was the Catechism of Saint Turibius of Mogrovejo.[46]

---

44   An American Indian ethnic group located in the Gran Chaco region of northern Argentina and southern Bolivia. —Ed.

45   In 1593, in the Argentinian city of La Rioja, the Diaguita Indians clashed with the colonial authorities over the Spanish mistreatment of the native population. The Franciscan missionary Saint Francis Solano, renowned among the people for his zeal as well as his violin playing, was called upon to negotiate peace, which he did—by castigating the Spaniards and declaring the Christ Child as mayor of the city. Ever since then, on the feast day of Saint Nicholas, patron saint of La Rioja, an elaborate, open-air liturgical celebration is held in the city to commemorate this event of reconciliation. The statue of Saint Nicholas is borne aloft from the cathedral and through the streets to meet the statue of the Christ Child, whereupon he genuflects three times before "Jesus the Mayor." —Ed.

46   Saint Turibius of Mogrovejo († 1606) was a layman serving as a judge at the court of Granada when King Philip II of Spain nominated him to succeed Jerome de Laoisa as archbishop of Lima, Peru. After strenuous but ultimately fruitless opposition to this decision, Turibius was swiftly ordained and sent to the New World at the age of thirty-nine. A great reformer and founder, he is responsible for the Catechism (written in Spanish and two native dialects, Quechua and Aymara) that contributed immensely to the

The memory of a people is not a computer hard drive, but *a heart*. Like Mary, peoples treasure things in their heart. In this regard, Spain has taught us to form firm bonds and faithfully remember the Lord, his Mother, and the saints, founding spiritual unity in our nations through them.

Memory is a unifying and integrating force. Thus, when interpersonal relations break down, memory is the only thing that can serve as cement to hold people and families together. A family without memory does not deserve such a name. A family that neither respects nor takes care of its grandparents, who are its living memory, is a shattered family. But a family and a people who exercise their memory are a true family and a people with a future.

All of mankind has a common memory. The memory of the ancestral battle between good and evil. The eternal combat between Michael and the Dragon, *"the ancient serpent"* (Rv 12:7-9), who has been conquered forever, yet who still rears his head as "the enemy of human nature" (*Sp. Ex.*, 136). *"How have you fallen from the heavens, O morning star, son of the dawn!"* prophesies Isaiah (14:12). *"Yet down to the nether world you go to the recesses of the pit!"* (v. 15). This is the memory of mankind, the bitter heritage shared

---

evangelization of South America. He fostered what came to be called the "great religious century" in Peru. Among those he influenced and confirmed are Saint Rose of Lima, Saint Martin de Porres, Saint John Macías, and Saint Mary Ann de Paredes. It is difficult to imagine the love this tireless apostle bore for the Indian people, whose devotion to him is profound. Canonized in 1726, Saint Turibius was proclaimed patron saint of the Latin American bishops in 1983 by Pope John Paul II. —Ed.

by all peoples and the revelation of God to Israel. Man's history is a protracted battle between grace and sin. Yet this common memory bears a concrete face: the face of the men and women who comprise our peoples. They are anonymous individuals whose names will not be recorded by history. Their faces will perhaps be marked by suffering and rejection, but their inexpressible dignity speaks to us of a people who have a history, a common memory. This is the faithful people of God.

The memory of the Church: the Passion of the Lord

Let us now consider the Lord's Passion. One of the antiphons for the feast of Corpus Christi, composed by Saint Thomas Aquinas, reads: "The memory of his Passion is recalled" (*recolitur memoria passionis eius*). The Eucharist is the memory of the Passion of the Lord. Here is the heart of the victory. The failure to remember this truth has sometimes made the Church appear triumphalist, but the Resurrection cannot be understood without the Cross. The history of the world is found in the Cross:

- grace and sin
- mercy and repentance
- good and evil
- time and eternity

The voice of God resounds in the ears of the Church, as expressed through the mouth of the Prophet: *"Fear not, for I have redeemed you...and I will come to rescue you again"* (cf. Is 43:1-21). *"Be brave and steadfast; have no fear or dread of them, for it is the LORD, your God, who marches with you; he will never fail you or forsake you.... So do not fear or be dismayed*" (Dt 31:6, 8). The memory of the salvation of God, of the distance already traveled, provides strength for the road ahead.

By means of her memory, the Church bears witness to the salvation of God. "*But do not be afraid of them. Rather call to mind what the LORD, your God, did to Pharaoh and all Egypt: the great testings which your own eyes have seen, the signs and wonders, with which the LORD, your God, brought you out. The same also he will do to all the nations of whom you are now afraid*" (Dt 7:18-19). The people of God were tested in the desert. They were guided by God like a son by his father. The counsel given in the Book of Deuteronomy is the same as in all of Scripture: "*Remember how...the LORD, your God, has directed all your journeying.... So you must know*" (Dt 8:2).

Nobody is able to understand anything if he is unable to remember well, if he lacks memory:

> *Take care and be earnestly on your guard not to forget the things your own eyes have seen, nor let them slip from your memory as long as you live, but teach them to your children and to your children's children.* (Dt 4:9)

Our God is jealous of the memory we have of him, so jealous that at the least sign of repentance, he becomes merciful, remembering "*the covenant which under oath he made with your fathers*" (Dt 4:31).

Moreover, whoever lacks memory turns to idols. Idol worship is the inherent punishment for those who forget (Dt 4:25-31), which in turn leads to slavery: "*Since* you would not serve the LORD, your God, with joy and gratitude for abundance of every kind, therefore in hunger and thirst, in nakedness and poverty, you will serve the enemies" (Dt 28:47-48). Memory alone enables us to discover God's presence in our midst and makes us realize that every attempt to seek salvation apart from God is an idol (Dt 6:14-15 and 7:17-26).

The Church remembers the mercies of God, and therefore tries to be faithful to the Law. The Ten Commandments we teach to our children are the other face of the Covenant, the juridical aspect that provides a human framework for God's mercy. When the people came forth from Egypt, it was a grace they received. And the Law is the complement to that received, the other side of the same coin. The commandments are the fruit of memory (Dt 6:1-12), and thus need to be transmitted from generation to generation:

> Later on, when your son asks you what these ordinances, statutes, and decrees mean which the LORD, our God, has enjoined on you, you shall say to your son, "We were once slaves of Pharaoh in Egypt, but the LORD brought us out of Egypt with his strong hand and wrought before our eyes signs and wonders, great and dire, against Egypt and against Pharaoh and his whole house. He brought us from there to lead us into the land he promised on oath to our fathers, and to give it to us. Therefore, the LORD commanded us to observe all these statutes in fear of the LORD, our God, that we may always have as prosperous and happy a life as we have today." (Dt 6:20-24)

Memory ties us to a tradition, a norm, a living law inscribed in the heart: "*Take these words of mine into your heart and soul. Bind them at your wrist as a sign"* (Dt 11:18). This is how God preserves in his heart and his whole being the "gift," the "project" of salvation.

The fundamental task of the Church, and of each one of us, to cultivate memory springs precisely from this assurance: the Lord remembers me, he binds me close to his heart. This is why prayer needs to be permeated with memory. It is the prayer of the Church that constantly keeps alive in the present the salvation of God the Father, accomplished through the Son, in the Holy Spirit. In the *Credo*, we do not only find a compendium of Christian truths, but also the history of our salvation: "born of the Virgin Mary," "suffered under Pontius Pilate," "was crucified," "rose again."

Our *Credo* is thus the prolongation and witness of the history of the faith of Israel that prayed in this way when presenting offerings to the Lord: *"My father was a wandering Aramean who went down to Egypt..... We cried to the LORD, the God of our fathers, and he heard our cry.... He brought us out of Egypt...and gave us this land"* (Dt 26:5-9). Memory is a grace that we must ask for. It is very easy to forget, especially when we are well fed.

> *When the LORD, your God, brings you into the land which he swore to your fathers, Abraham, Isaac and Jacob, that he would give to you, a land with fine, large cities that you did not build, with houses full of goods of all sorts that you did not garner, with cisterns that you did not dig, with vineyards and olive groves that you did not plant; and when, therefore, you eat your fill, take care not to forget the LORD, who brought you out of the land of Egypt, that place of slavery.* (Dt 6:10-12)

> *Be careful not to forget the LORD, your God, by neglecting his commandments and decrees and statutes which I enjoin on you today: lest, when you have eaten your fill, and have built fine houses and lived in them, and have increased your herds and flocks, your silver and gold, and all your property, you then become haughty of heart and unmindful of the LORD, your God, who brought you out of the land of Egypt, that place of slavery.* (Dt 8:11-14)

Let us beg for the grace of memory, in order to know how to make the right choice between life and death: *"See, I have today set before you life and good, death and evil"* (Dt 30:15-20; see also 11:26 and all of chapter 28). We must make this choice between the Lord and idols on a daily basis. This memory will also make us merciful because we will hear this great truth in our heart: *"Remember that you too were once slaves in Egypt"* (Dt 15:15).

And may the Lord grant his Church the grace that he bestowed upon Moses, the guide of our memory: *"His eyes were undimmed and his vigor unabated"* (Dt 34:7). Provided that our modern idols, which never have a history but are always merely "present," do not deprive us of the vision of memory! Let us hold fast to our first love (Jer 2:1-13). May we never hear the words the Lord spoke to the angel of the Church of Ephesus: *"Yet I hold this against you: you have lost the love you had at first"* (Rv 2:4).

The Virgin Mary, who *"treasured all these things and reflected on them in her heart"* (Lk 2:19), will teach us the grace of memory if we know how to ask for it in humility. She, like the mother in the Book of Maccabees, will know how to speak to us in our "mother tongue" (cf. 2 Mc 7:21-

26), the language of our fathers, which we learned how to speak in the "*pristinos dies*" ("the former days," Heb 10:32). May we never go without the affection and tenderness of Mary who whispers the word of God in our ears, in the mother tongue of our family. Then we will receive the power to turn a deaf ear to the blandishments of the Evil One, and walk away laughing.

The Bride of the Lord

His commandment is this: we are to believe in the name of his Son, Jesus Christ, and are to love one another as he commanded. (1 Jn 3:23)

Jesus *founds* the Church, and he *founds us* in the Church.

The mystery of the Church is intimately bound to the mystery of Mary, the Mother of God and the Mother of the Church. Mary gives birth to us and takes care of us. So does the Church. Mary makes us grow. So does the Church. And at the hour of death, the priest accompanies us in the name of the Church, committing us to Mary's embrace. "*A woman clothed with the sun, with the moon under her feet, and on her head a crown of twelve stars*" (Rv 12:1). This is the Church, and this is the Church our faithful people revere. Therefore, when we speak about the Church, we need to feel the same devotion as we do for the Virgin Mary. "Our holy Mother, the hierarchical Church" (*Sp. Ex.*, 353), such was the expression Saint Ignatius held dear. This same expression evokes three interconnected concepts:

- holiness
- fecundity
- discipline

We are born for holiness in a holy body, that of our holy Mother the Church. Both our vocation to be "holy and irreproachable in his sight" (cf. Col 1:22) and our apostolic fruitfulness depend upon our disciplined desire to live in loving communion with this Body.

The Church is holy: she remains in the world "as a sign—simultaneously obscure and luminous—of a new presence of Jesus, of his departure and of his permanent presence. She prolongs and continues him" (*E.N.*, 15). Her holiness—"the life of prayer, of listening to the Word and the apostles' teaching, charity lived in a fraternal way, the sharing of bread—this intimate life only acquires its full meaning when it becomes a witness, when it evokes admiration and conversion, and when it becomes the preaching and proclamation of the Good News" (*ibid.*). Her holiness is not naïve: "She is the People of God immersed in the world, and often tempted by idols, and she always needs to hear the proclamation of the 'mighty works of God' [cf. Acts 2:11; 1 Pt 2:9] which converted her to the Lord; she always needs to be called together afresh by him" (*ibid.*).

The Fathers of the Church captured this mystery of the holiness of the Church tempted by idols in the term *casta meretrix* (chaste harlot). The holiness of the Church is reflected in the face of Mary, who is without sin, pure and without blemish; but she does not forget that within her womb she also bears the children of Eve, mother of sinful mankind.

The Church possesses a vast and rich theological tradition of holiness, and for her canonizations she draws upon this wisdom—with the unfailing aid of the Holy Spirit—while making use of established criteria that are familiar to all of us. In our clerical "patois" we sometimes joke about the sometimes fastidious use of the term "holy," and so we say, with a smile, "this holy house," "these holy customs." But it is also true that when we want to offer a definitive judgment—with joy—about someone, and we say, "That man was a saint," it is as if we are dropping our idols and getting down on our knees before the mystery of God and his infinite goodness that inhabited this man.

Love and devotion to our Mother the Church corresponds to love and devotion to each of her children in particular. And we have many saints in the Church—we are in contact with holy people every day: in parish life, in the confessional, in spiritual direction. I often ask myself whether the bitter criticism of the Church, the pain and disappointment over her many sins, and the sense of hopelessness it tends to create in us, are not directly related to the fact that we are undernourished. That is, because we do not avail ourselves enough of this proximity to the Church's lived holiness, which is a reconciling presence, for it is God visiting his Body.

Holiness, fecundity, and evangelical zeal

Just as there is an intrinsic link between holiness and the maternity of the Church, so there is also an intrinsic link between our holiness as consecrated men and our fecundity in founding and forming Christian hearts. That is to say, holiness bears fruit in us through our apostolic zeal:

> Our evangelizing zeal must spring from true holiness of life, and, as the Second Vatican Council suggests, preaching must in its turn make the preacher grow in holiness, which is nourished by prayer and above all by love for the Eucharist. (*E.N.*, 76)

In this context, we can reflect on the specific questions Paul VI poses to us, knowing that we are all responsible for the answers:

> "What is the state of the Church [fifty] years after the Council?"…. Is she firmly established in the midst of the world and yet free and independent enough to call for the world's attention? Does she testify to solidarity with people and at the same time to the divine Absolute? Is she more ardent in contemplation and adoration and more zealous in missionary, charitable and liberating action? Is she ever more committed to the effort to search for the restoration of the complete unity of Christians, a unity that makes more effective the common witness, "so that the world may believe" [Jn 17:21]? (*E.N.*, 76)

To speak about our holy Mother the Church evokes the gift of *fecundity*. Often we can become skeptical about hoping in fecundity, like Sarah who laughed to herself when she was promised a son. On the other hand, we can sometimes react with euphoria and start wanting to quantify and plan everything out, thus repeating the sin of David whose vanity led him to take a census of the people.

The fruitfulness of the Gospel follows other paths. It is like the certitude that the Lord will not abandon us and will keep his promise to stay with us until the end of the world. This is a paradoxical fecundity: to be fruitful, yet at the same time not to be self-conscious about it. All the while not being completely unaware of it either!

I remember the words of an Argentinian priest, Father Matías Crespí, a tireless missionary in Patagonia. When he was old he made this quip, "My life just flew right by," meaning that in his estimation he had accomplished little for the Lord. This is the fecundity of the dew that moistens without making a sound. It is the fecundity founded upon a faith that asks for evidence, but which accepts that such evidence is not definitive. This is the evidence of the Lord's presence, which consoles us (*Sp. Ex.*, 224), fortifying our faith, and then leaves us to carry on with our mission as stewards, to wait in fidelity "until he comes again."

The Church is a mother. She gives birth to sons and daughters with the power of the deposit of faith. She is "the depositary of the Good News to be proclaimed. The promises of the New Alliance in Jesus Christ, the teaching of the Lord and the apostles, the Word of life, the sources of grace and of God's loving kindness, the path of salvation — all these things have been entrusted to her. It is the content of the Gospel, and therefore of evangelization, that she preserves as a precious living heritage, not in order to keep it hidden but to communicate it" (*E.N.*, 15), which is to say, to beget life! She gives birth to children in constant fidelity to her Spouse, in order to send them out "to preach not their own selves or their personal ideas [cf. 2 Cor 4:5], but a Gospel of which neither she nor they are the absolute masters and owners, to dispose of it as they wish, but a Gospel of which they are the ministers, in order to pass it on with complete fidelity" (*ibid.*). The fidelity she bears for her faithful Spouse educates us in our faithful fecundity.

To want to be fruitful is a legitimate desire, but the Gospel has its own laws for legitimizing our activities. It is like saying, you will be fruitful:

    – if you jealously defend your condition as a simple worker

    – if you harmonize diligence with the awareness that you are useless

    – if, deep down, you admit that your task is to plow the earth and sow the seed, while irrigating and harvesting are graces that belong to the Lord

We have to love the mystery of the Church's fecundity just as we love the mystery of Mary, Virgin and Mother. In the light of this love, let us love the mystery of our role as useless servants, with the hope that the Lord will one day speak these words to us: "*Well done, my good and faithful servant*" (Mt 25:21, 23).

Our love for the Church is the love of a union with a Body, and this demands *discipline*. We can express this by saying that, in a certain way, it corresponds to the formula *discreta caritas* (charity filled with discretion). For a priest or bishop to lack discipline means to lack discretion, which is always a lack of love.

Discrete love allows us to be "fully conscious of belonging to a large community which neither space nor time can limit" (*E.N.*, 61). This sense of belonging helps us to understand and embrace the mission we have received, the mission to evangelize:

> Evangelization is for no one an individual and isolated act; it is one that is deeply ecclesial. When the most obscure preacher, catechist or pastor in the most distant land preaches the Gospel, gathers his little community together or administers a sacrament, even alone, he is carrying out an ecclesial act, and his action is certainly attached to the evangelizing activity of the whole Church by institutional relationships, but also by profound invisible links in the order of grace. This presupposes that he acts not in virtue of a mission which he attributes to himself or by a personal inspiration, but in union with the mission of the Church and in her name. (*E.N.*, 60)

Thus, our discipline is rooted in the awareness that:

> no evangelizer is the absolute master of his evangelizing action, with a discretionary power to carry it out in accordance with individualistic criteria and perspectives; he acts in communion with the Church and her pastors. (*ibid.*)

Our adherence to the Kingdom, "which cannot remain abstract and unincarnated, reveals itself concretely by a visible entry into a community of believers...the Church, the visible sacrament of salvation" (*E.N.*, 23). Adherence to the Kingdom thus means:

> communion with the visible sign of the encounter with God which is the Church of Jesus Christ; and this communion in its turn is expressed by the application of those other signs of Christ living and acting in the Church which are the sacraments. (*E.N.*, 28)

Our adherence to the Kingdom, therefore, leads us into ever deeper communion with the Bridegroom, into the very side of Christ asleep on the Cross, from which his Spouse is born, the fruitful Mother of a disciplined Body nourished by the sacraments.

> There is thus a profound link between Christ, the Church and evangelization. During the period of the Church that we are living in, it is she who has the task of evangelizing. This mandate is not accomplished without her, and still less against her. (*E.N.*, 16)

It is an "absurd dichotomy" to pretend to "to love Christ but without the Church, to listen to Christ but not the Church, to belong to Christ but outside the Church" (*ibid.*).

Discipline is neither a kind of badge or decoration, nor is it a type of training in good manners. An undisciplined heart can eventually emerge in the form of the *hombre turba* (disturbed or agitated man) whom Saint Ignatius talks about, those who have not mastered their passions. As a result, they can sow discord and division, resort to betrayal in order to gain followers, establish unjust social structures in the heart of a community or diocese through a continuous pharisaical attitude.

My aim in this meditation was to speak on the love for "our holy Mother the hierarchical Church." We have become aware that it is our responsibility to be children of the Church, and at the same time to be the Church. Our love of the Church should lead us to give witness before the world, to witness to her holiness, to her warm fecundity, and to her discipline that is to be entirely